Free Your Mind... Release Your Dreams

A step-by-step guide to changing your life through self hypnosis

Tim Hodgson

FREE YOUR MIND

Copyright © Tim Hodgson 2008

ISBN 978-1-4357-4371-7

Published by Lulu

Free Your Mind... Release Your Dreams

First Published July 2008

This book is dedicated to David & Jonny, whose love and support have helped me build the life and career I have always dreamed of. I am proud to have you as my friends.

ACKNOWLEDGEMENTS

There have been so many friends, colleagues, companions and fellow adventurers in my life that I feel so much of a debt of gratitude to.

In particular, my thanks go to my hypnotherapy trainer, Topher Morrison, and all those who have been part of that journey and adventure, and especially Jen Woolley for her willingness to experience my hypnotic skills! Roy Martin, Julie Palfrey and the Joy For Life team have been responsible, too, for so much of my learning about the power of meditation. And my thanks, too, to those who encouraged me to use the power of my voice to teach, to train, and to help people – and especially to Monique Oxley for her belief and faith in me.

There are so many people who have touched my life through their writings, but in particular my thanks to Joe Vitale, Dr Ihaleakala Hew Len, Neale Donald Walsch, Eckhart Tolle and Marianne Williamson for showing me so much of what is possible when we truly open our lives up to the power of the Divine.

There are so many, many others whose incredible trainings, coaching, books, newsletters, and websites I have devoured. Thank you for leading me, and teaching me, and helping me to grow into all I can possibly be.

And to my friends and peers – in particular Rachael Land, David Warren, Gary Cousins, Jen Woolley and a host of wonderful and amazing people that I've met on my travels. Thank you for your love, and for holding me to a higher standard. There are three people who have continually believed in me, provoked me and acted as my support team – Mandy Holloway, Sue Gorringe and Yve Rowse. And also thanks to Heather Lewis, who apart from being the best dance partner a man could dream of has also been instrumental in pushing me forward, in believing in me, and in giving me a good kick where it's needed. Thankyou.

And, of course, my thanks go to my family and especially to my incredible sons, and my best friends and true heroes, David and Jonny, for supporting me as I wrote this programme. I'm truly proud of you, guys. I'd also like to thank the rest of Team Hodgson for their love and support – especially Chris who managed to survive being my younger brother and has taught me so much about love and responsibility.

ADDITIONAL RESOURCES

We've made some special audio resources available on line for you to use with this manual. These will help you get familiar with the hypnosis process, and will mean that you don't need to relax and read at the same time! There's a list of the different audios and a web link to them in the section on 'Further Resources' at the end of the manual, but so you can find them easily, I've also marked the sections available as audio with the symbol ◀┊

FROM THE AUTHOR

"And all creation stands on tiptoe just to see the sons of God come into their own"

- St Paul, Romans 8v19

Life is an adventure. Life is designed to be exciting, thrilling, joyful, full of exploration and discovery. Life is designed to be enjoyed. What I have set out to do is to give you some tools that will help you enjoy that life even more. I've wanted to share with you some of my experience that I have learnt on my own journey – some of the beliefs and understandings that help me in creating the life I want to have, and the adventure that I am currently enjoying.

My goal throughout all that I do is to let you know that you can. Whatever it is. You can live the life you want. You can have the success that you want. You can have the relationships that you want. You can have the experiences that you want. That's why you are on this planet – so you can have what, at a deep, spiritual level, what you want and what you are prepared to experience. It's as simple as that.

When I coach people I am not focussed on their goals, what they want to achieve, what their plans are, what obstacles they face. I'm not looking to help them meet their deadlines and nag them when they don't. I'm not even looking to help them understand their balance between personal and business life. I want them to know that they CAN. They can do what they want. They can live the dreams they want. They can have the lifestyle they want.

I wish I could communicate in some way how much that passion beats in me – how much I long to be able to explain in some way that whatever the question is, YOU are the answer to it. It is my lifelong dream to see the sons of God come into their own, and to see each and every member of the human race grow and evolve. I hope this programme will help.

You are unique, you are incredible, and you have an amazing gift to bring to the world – one that only you can give. If I can in any way help you to bring that gift out into the open, for you to live your adventure, your journey, and live the life you have dreamed of, then I will have done my job.

So, buckle up, and get ready for the adventure of your life....

Chapter 1

BEFORE YOU START

"As I grow to understand life less and less, I learn to love it more and more."

- Jules Renard, French author

This is a journey into the science of the 'spooky'. The approved technical term for this is 'weird stuff'. In this modern age we've learnt to accept that which we can see, touch, feel. We've learnt to trust our senses and only our senses – that which can be demonstrated and proved physically. Our scientific world has taught us the importance of verifying results, and has cautioned us to be suspicious of those things that we can't directly verify.

Somehow our ancestors had more faith in the unseen. A lot of what they believed, of course, was wildly superstitious, but they did have an absolute belief in the power of the invisible.

With hypnosis, no-one really knows how it works. There is so much progress being made on the workings of the mind and of consciousness, but most of it is, to be honest, an educated guess. We make a lot of assumptions, and we try hard to work out what's going on in our heads, but in the end all we can do is to look at the results we get and make our own minds up.

And let's face it, that's what the scientists are doing too. They are basing their knowledge of distant stars on the observable effects that we can see here. They base their knowledge of the inner workings of the atom on the effects that they can see in the things around, and not actually by observing the atoms themselves... so, in truth, they are also making guesses based on what they observe.

I'm going to give you as much information as I can to help you make your mind up for yourself. I'm going to give you the opportunity to try this out for yourself and see how it works for you. In the end, that's all that matters, of course. It's actually the core question that scientists use when they develop complex experiments to prove their theories: "Does it work?" In the end, while it might be nice to know *how* something works, it isn't necessary to know for us to use it. Like me, you probably don't know how television works – but we can enjoy using it.

I can remember Margaret Thatcher, who was then the UK Prime Minister, proudly proclaiming during a visit to a semiconductor fabrication plant back in the late 1970s "Everyone else is talking about the microchip – but I can say I understand it." Sorry to burst your balloon, Maggie, but I'm afraid that there were only three men at the time that had a reasonable idea of what was going on in the quantum physics of microelectronics. Hey, I spent three years studying microelectronics at degree level and I didn't understand it!

I'm also reminded of a conversation with one of the broadcast TV engineers responsible for the transmission stations for terrestrial TV, where he confessed that he had no idea what some of the components on the circuit boards in the transmission stations actually DID. They weren't even connected. But when they took them away, the transmitter stopped working.

It's the same with the science of the human mind. We don't really understand how it works, but we can still use what we know to get the results that we want. This manual will help you do just that.

Now, a lot of the work that I do is involved with the conscious and unconscious mind – with the sciences of hypnotherapy, Neuro-Linguistic Programming, and psychology. I've worked with many, many people to help them get the results that they want through therapy work and through coaching. Simply by working with their imaginations, their belief systems, and their physiology, I've been able to help them to create massive change for themselves. They've been able to go from being blown about by everything going on around them to being the cause of everything that happens in their lives.

I'd like to point out that in all the work I have done with people I have only been a guide. The real work is down to the person themselves. As I will say over and over again in this manual – the responsibility for change is on your own shoulders. The programming is inside you, and only you can choose to change it. Now that's incredibly powerful, if you think about it. You don't need coaches, you don't need teachers, you don't even need hypnotherapists or NLP practitioners, counsellors or psychologists. This manual will help put the tools in your hands that will help create massive change for you. If you want it.

That's one of the reasons I've not included many scripts in this manual. I've read many books with hypnotherapy scripts in them, and while they are great to model, there's nothing that compares to developing a set of affirmations for yourself. When I look at other people's scripts I spend a lot of time trying to work out how they've made the connection between the metaphor and the problem (I'm particularly fond of one example on sexual performance using a firehose as a metaphor). They tend also to be a bit inflexible – and you're different from everyone else, aren't you? Even when working one to one with people I take great care to match the metaphor and the suggestions to the person – so I don't think that handing you a pre-canned set of scripts and affirmations is going to help you much. I'd rather you had something that will work for you, that you've been involved in creating. So if you will forgive me – I'd like to leave the stories and the metaphors up to you.

Finally, I'd like to mention that recently I have also been discovering a spiritual dimension to the work I do. It seems that the more we discover, the more we find out, then many of our leading scientific minds are admitting that there is something beyond our knowledge. Whatever it is, there is something out there that our physics, our mathematics and our science can't quite explain. I'm no different – when I start to look closely at humanity, it seems that I have to include a spiritual aspect.

For many of my readers, that will be fine – at some level they agree with me. For others, while they can accept the scientific concepts behind hypnosis, the spiritual aspects are one step too far. Here's the thing… that's perfectly OK. Throughout this programme, simply decide what works for you. I want you to take responsibility for what you learn and what you experience. All I ask is that you have an open mind, use your own judgement, and accept what works for you and fits your belief system. And whatever doesn't – well, just keep an open mind, but it's OK to believe what you want to.

So let's get cracking – let's start the exploration, and let's see just how far into Wonderland this particular rabbit hole goes[1], and what adventures we can have as we follow.

---

[1] My thanks to Lewis Carroll and the white rabbit of 'Alice in Wonderland'

Chapter 2

THE ART OF THE POSSIBLE

Miracles don't really require a belief in magic, just a disbelief in limits. At which point there's little you can do to stem their tide.

— Mike Dooley of www.tut.com

Where do we start? In the 21st century we are only just starting to understand the power of the mind. John Hagelin, one of the stars of the movie 'The Secret' says that scientists don't even know what the source of consciousness is, or where it is located. There are certainly some studies that suggest that consciousness and 'the mind' is not located in the brain at all, but is distributed around the body. The spine, the nervous system, and every single nerve seem to be part of the consciousness process.

Other studies seem to indicate that the function of consciousness is not necessarily located in the body at all, and may extend around it. This might even be an explanation of the 'aura' that some people see around others. I've certainly done experiments myself that demonstrate some form of electrical field around the body.

Scientists will now point out that we are all actually energy. What we perceive as solid is of course just a collection of atoms held together by energy – it's the fact that these atoms repel each other that prevents us walking through doors (damn – I've always wanted to do that). If you look really closely, the world – and that includes you and me - is actually mostly empty space, mostly made up of the gaps between atoms.

Look a little closer, and you find that even those atoms start to look like 'thickened up energy'. They don't really exist. It seems clear that really we are energy that appears solid. Now that we understand that, then the possibility that we are all in some way connected and part of a larger and greater interconnected consciousness seems more than a remote possibility. Lynne McTaggart has written an eye opening book called 'The Field' which goes into this much more than we have time for here – see the chapter 'Continuing the Adventure' for more information on pursuing some of these intriguing concepts.

Whatever the truth, it's fairly clear that we are only using a small fraction of the mind's capabilities. Many scientists seem to suggest that we might be effectively using maybe 5% of its capacity. I'm not even sure it's that high – it seems to me that you and I use our minds very poorly. Can you imagine what it would be like if we really could use our brains effectively? What would you be able to achieve if you could think more clearly, learn more effectively, remember with more clarity? What would happen if you could change the negative and unhelpful programming and install new programs that gave you the results you want in your life? Would that be cool?

Now, I'm not going to get into advanced memory techniques, or rapid reading, or advanced learning in this programme. There are more than enough of those programmes out there. What I do want to do is to look at how you can use the power of self hypnosis to create massive changes in your life.

We're going to look at how you can set the power of your unconscious mind free to solve problems that you can't solve consciously. We're going to look at ways to boost your auto-immune system to give you increased health and vitality.

We'll explore how you can use self hypnosis for relaxation and to reduce stress. We'll look at how a simply hypnotic programme that you can learn quickly and easily can give you a rapid refresher in a few moments, leaving you full of energy.

We're also going to take a look at how self hypnosis can connect you to the universe, exploring some of the spiritual dimensions and how self hypnosis is closely aligned with meditation. We'll also investigate how self hypnosis might even open up extra sensory powers, giving you a new sense of what's possible in the world.

How does that sound? Well, strap yourself in, and let's begin your adventure into the power of what's possible....

Chapter 3

SPECIAL POWERS WOULD BE SO COOL

"Flame On!"

- Jonnie Storm in 'The Fantastic Four'

When I was younger, I was always caught in class daydreaming.... The teacher used to despair of me, as my attention wandered yet again to some incredible world where anything was possible – where any of your dreams can come true. I often used to dream of being a superhero, like in the comic books. It was incredible – just imagine, they seemed to be able to do anything. Any problem that you could think of, they could solve – just zoom in and anything was possible. I used to long to have some super powers of my own, you know.

I used to love the Human Torch – when he was on fire he could fly, and he tended to ignite anything that was around him. Or Cyclops, whose eyes would blaze with power, sweeping away anything that got in his way. Or Storm, who could control the elements and the weather, who could change what was happening in the world around her. I used to love DareDevil too. DareDevil was blind, but his other senses had become so incredibly powerful that he could sense what was going on without being able to see – he was almost magically aware of his environment.

It's odd, considering that I eventually ended up studying the science of the mind, but one of my favourites was Professor X from the X men. He had this incredible ability to use his mind to do some really amazing things, and I used to wonder what it would be like to have that sort of power – you know, to be able to use your mind to achieve whatever you wanted. "Wouldn't that be cool", I used to think to myself, "wouldn't it be fabulous to be able to help people simply by using the power of the mind?"

One of my all time heroes is the wizard Merlin. He influenced a nation and an entire generation with his magic. Legends and myths surround the man, and of course we have no real idea of who the real Merlin was. There is something in Merlin and Arthur that calls to all of us.

I often sit back and chill out and imagine what it was like back then, in a different world and a different time. A time of incredible poverty, with smoke drifting across the landscape from a myriad cooking pots and open fires, a time of wildness and lawlessness, a time of great poverty and fear. And yet, a time of great opportunity, when anything could happen, where nothing was quite what it seemed, where power was hidden in the humblest of vessels. Remember that Arthur was just a poor serving lad, the lowest of the low.. who had been offered a chance of a lifetime to be the squire for Sir Kay, one of the knights of the realm. Something was already calling our hero – events that would have massive implications for him, for his nation, and for history. Arthur's impact was to stretch far beyond the movies, far beyond Disney, far beyond the tales that are told: somehow it touches all of us.

Arthur's arrival at court coincided with a tremendous uproar in the castle. Everywhere around people were rushing to and fro, lord and commoner alike were fighting to see what was going on. At the centre of a ring of people stood the great sword, embedded up to its hilt in rock. Rumours went round – that someone would be able to pull the sword from the stone, would be able to wield its power, would be allowed to rule, would be able to tame the wildness at the heart of the nation.

A little way away, warming his hands around a campfire, sat a man almost hidden by his beard and cloak. But his eyes were bright as he watched the scene unfolding in front of him. There seemed to be something almost unworldly about him – almost as if he was the centre of the events that had captured everyone's interest – as if the world revolved around this one man, and not around the sword, and the rock, and the kitchen lad who, to the shocked amazement of the crowd, had pulled the sword from the stone.

In one swift movement Merlin crossed to where Arthur stood, holding the sword that told of a power greater than he could have imagined. As he drew him aside, he spoke calmly and yet with great authority: "You have a great power there, in your hands – maybe a greater power than you can imagine. You have the chance to rise from where you are, to change your stars – and to change the face of the nation. You have the chance to reclaim your destiny, your birthright, your truth. Are you prepared to learn… to discover… to remember Who You Truly Are?"

Chapter 4

ON WITH THE ADVENTURE

'The dream is real, Neo'

-Morpheus in 'The Matrix'

So, what is it you want to achieve with self hypnosis? Perhaps you want to learn to relax and eliminate stress. Perhaps you want to be able to activate your unconscious mind to help you solve problems and get answers to your challenges as if by magic. Perhaps you'd like to rewire your brain to be able to give up smoking, or lose weight. Maybe you'd like to be able to get a fast start on meditation and spiritual practice. It's all possible, you know… in fact, anything is possible.

What we're doing with self hypnosis is to help you to free up the latent power of your mind. We're helping you to find ways to access and communicate with a part of your consciousness that's largely gone unnoticed – quietly working away day after day, achieving minor miracles of learning, response, creativity and self preservation. We're going to learn how to learn how to operate as a single mind, to unleash connections that you never thought you had, to tap into resources that you simply weren't aware of.

Who knows where that journey will take you: you see, that's entirely up to you. You can use your new found power to change your life. You could get in touch with a whole new level of creativity that you didn't know you'd got, using the power of your whole mind to come up with new solutions to problems. Maybe you're looking to reach a new level of health and wholeness. Maybe you're looking for the bigger answers, looking to explore the possibilities of abilities beyond normal comprehension, discovering the supernormal. And maybe, just maybe, you'll discover how to touch the Divine, to connect to the power in the Universe...

The possibilities and opportunities are absolutely incredible, you know.

So follow me on the adventure in Wonderland – and let's see just how far that rabbit hole goes...

Chapter 5

SO WHAT *IS* HYPNOSIS ANYWAY?

"The best reason for having dreams is that in dreams no reasons are necessary."

Ashleigh Brilliant (English Author and Cartoonist)

It's probably worth spending a little while looking at the history of hypnosis, just so you get an idea of its legacy and to see it as a legitimate way to improve your mind.

Many people think that hypnosis is a recent idea, but in fact way back in Egypt around 2000BC the Pharaoh Imhotep used to have 'Temples of Sleep' which were used to cure patients. People used to go into the temple to sleep, and come out miraculously cured. Could it be that the suggestion of "you're going to be healed" coupled with the relaxing trance in the temple and the recognition of the king and priest as an expert led to the healing?

Fast forward to 1500 AD (or thereabouts) and Paracelsus was mucking about with magnets – healing people with magnetic fields. In fact, we still have magnet therapy today. Fast forward again to the early 1800s, and Franz Mesmer was still using magnets to treat his patients. He'd get them laid down and relaxed (sounding familiar yet?) and pass magnets over the affected part. One day, our hero forgot to bring his magnets. Not to be dismayed, of course (and probably not to miss out on getting paid) he did exactly the same thing but without the magnets. He was somewhat surprised to find that he got exactly the same results without the magnets. He realised that the relaxed state coupled with the suggestion of getting well had produced a healing state in the client – and 'Mesmerism' was born.

Over the years the field of hypnosis was further developed. James Braid, a Scotsman, was actually the first to coin the word 'hypnotism' in his work with what he referred to as 'neurypnology'. Meanwhile, his colleague Esdaile had produced dramatic improvements in the survival rates of war injuries in India, raising the chances of survival from a depressing 50/50 chance to over 90% likelihood of surviving.

Later patrons of the field in the first part of the 20th century included Sigmund Freud, who apparently had developed such bad breath that he tended to do his hypnotism without looking at the patient at all, and Ivan Pavlov (he of "Pavlov's dogs" fame).

Many consider Milton Erickson to be the father of modern day hypnosis – dispensing with the swinging watch chain, Erickson would simply talk his patients into a trance state through his use of 'artfully vague' language and utilisation of everything that happened in a session to convince the patient to relax and let go of their conscious control over their minds. Erickson's language patterns became a core part of the technology of Neuro-Linguistic programming, and still rank today as incredible tools to create trance states. It's worthwhile investigating some of Milton Erickson's work, and looking at the linguistic model that bears his name, the Milton Model, which is chock full of hypnotic language patterns.

Eventually the American and British medical societies decided to (somewhat grudgingly) accept hypnotism as a valid therapy, and the modern hypnotherapist's career was assured.

So here's the thing. Hypnosis is accepted as a valid and powerful way of creating change, of relaxing, of helping people to achieve their goals – an incredibly useful tool for the psychologist and the doctor alike.

But do we actually NEED a hypnotherapist? If the goal of the hypnotist is simply to relax the client and to give the client empowering suggestions that enable change, consider this. What if we did the hypnosis ourselves? What if we cut out the middle man? Now wouldn't THAT be very cool?

Chapter 6

THE FINAL FRONTIER

We're really now moving into a new era. It's the era where the last frontier is not Space, as Star Trek would say, but it's going to be Mind

- Fred Alan Wolf, US quantum physicist

It's incredible that we know more about the surface of the moon than we do about the workings of the human mind... and it's also really exciting to be at the front of developments in what may prove to be the most incredible set of scientific discoveries ever. When we work with the human mind we are exploring a new world, a place where normal limitations seem to disappear and it's possible to achieve anything at all.

OK, HOW DOES THIS HYPNOSIS STUFF WORK THEN?

Simply put, hypnosis works by relaxing the mind so that hypnotic suggestions are readily accepted. Because the body and the mind are connected (you don't get one without the other) then relaxing the body will relax the mind. That's all there is to it. So let's take a quick look at what's going on in our minds – and then we'll dig into even more of what the mind us up to every moment of the day.

EXPLORING YOUR MIND

Let's start out looking at the package deal you got as a member of the human race. And, in particular, consider the incredibly powerful consciousness that defines who 'you' are. You're not your body, you see – you're more than that, aren't you? You're not even your mind – you're more than that, too. In fact, I have no words to explain just how incredible a being you are – capable of incredible thought, brilliant creativity, inspiring love and heartfelt feelings.

So I just want that to be running through you right now – there are no limits to what you can do, who you can be, what you can achieve. You are full of incredible possibilities. **The only limits are the ones that we place on ourselves.** And, honestly, that's the key. I want you to get excited by the possibilities that YOU have, and curious to see just what you can achieve when you start to really make use of the potential of your whole mind.

So let's look at the human mind for a moment. Consider this – your mind is powerful enough to take the millions of pieces of information that are thrown at it every second of every day and judge what's important and what isn't. You can see patterns in that whirl of information and make decisions based on what you see. You can compare the current situation with what you've experienced before and decide what to do. What's more, you can take that information and experience and **you can predict what's going to happen in the future**.

Your incredible being keeps you alive without you even thinking about it. You can walk and breathe and move without having to concentrate on each step and each action. In fact, you can set your unconscious mind a task and it will go away and achieve that task without you having to be involved at all! Have you ever had one of those moments when the answer to a problem has leapt almost unbidden into your mind? That's your unconscious mind at work solving problems while you get on and do something else. Some authorities suggest that we're using 5% at the most of our mind's capability – based on measuring what parts of the brain 'light up'. I suspect that figure is an exaggeration, and it's actually even less than that.

Other studies that suggest that consciousness and thought are not even confined to the brain itself, but seem to stretch throughout the nervous system and actually beyond the boundaries of the body itself. It's odd, but in some ways we know more about the surface of the moon than we do about the way our own minds work!

So let's start by looking at the way the mind is structured. Relax – I'm not going to go into the complex biology of the brain, or a detailed analysis of the nervous system. We're just going to use a simple model of the mind that will help us to understand what's going on – and how hypnosis works.

Even the ancients believe that the mind was composed of three parts. The Hawaiians referred to these as

Unhipili	the unconscious mind
Uhane	the conscious mind
Aumakua	the superconscious mind

Now, I'm not suggesting that there are necessarily three parts, and I'm well aware of the brain research that splits the brain into logical left hemisphere and create right hemisphere, or, using a different model, into different components based on their relationship to things like motor functions. I'm talking at a deeper and more holistic level than that, based on the behaviour that we observe.

I would guess that the **conscious mind** is the part of our thinking process that we're most aware of. It's the conscious mind that's making decisions, processing logically, doing calculations, finding solutions. It's the conscious mind that you can hear chattering in your head as you try and work out the best course of action. The conscious mind really acts as a control program that controls the rest of the mind – in fact, it's a bit like an auditor, controlling what's going on in the conscious mind, making sure it doesn't misbehave.

Every year or so when I worked in a large corporate we would have the auditors round, checking that we were doing what we should, whether we were following the rules or not. Often we used to think that some of the rules they came up with were completely daft – but without the auditor absolute chaos would rule as we would have got away with anything we wanted to. So control was a good thing – and yet it did sometimes stop us creating the changes that we wanted to. Now the way we got round the auditor was to give him something else to worry about to act as a diversion – which meant that the small changes we needed could be implemented while he wasn't looking.

Our job in self hypnosis or in hypnotherapy is to get the conscious mind out of the way – to occupy the auditor with a distraction or three while we give the unconscious mind new programming. In this programme we'll explore some ways you can do exactly that... or at least to get the auditor to nip down the pub for lunch.

What's more, the conscious mind seems to have a limited capacity, only doing one thing at once. Much like a modern computer, it simulates doing several things at once by swapping tasks rapidly in rotation. It's a bit like that old circus act of plate spinning – by attending to each plate in rotation, the juggler can keep several plates spinning – but eventually, as the number of plates to juggle gets too high, they start to crash to the ground.

Authorities suggest this limit is between 5 and 10 things at a time. Conventional wisdom suggests, of course, that men can actually only think about one thing at a time. Having thought about this for a while, I decided that we needed more conclusive evidence of this hypothesis. After extensive research and a full experimental trial, my own experiments have conclusively demonstrated that even men can definitely think of five things at a time: 'sex', 'food', 'TV', 'sport' and 'even more sex'.

Keep this in mind – the limit on the number of things you can do is one of the ways that hypnosis works, by overloading the conscious mind so that it 'gives up' and has to let the unconscious take over. Simply by giving the conscious mind lots of things to do – resolving ambiguity, comparing truth to reality, creating pictures, etc etc, the conscious mind's 'buffer' gets overloaded. One result of this overload is that the conscious mind goes into a trance.

Derren Brown used to do a segment on his show where someone would pass a public phone box that was ringing. The unsuspecting passer-by would pick up the phone, listen for a moment and then fall asleep on the spot, slumped by the call box or slowly collapsing down the wall onto the floor. On the other end of the phone, apparently, Derren was throwing all sorts of suggestions at them – confusing their minds so that they looked for anything that they could understand, and completely overloading the conscious mind. When the command came "Sleep now" the poor victim would hear it unconsciously and simply fall asleep – obeying the only instruction that actually made sense.

The conscious mind would like to think that it's in charge. It's probably wrong most of the time.

The **unconscious mind**, on the other hand, is the part of your mind that actually runs the show day to day. It's the unconscious mind that handles the processes like breathing, reacting, actually running your body. It's the unconscious mind that handles all the complexities of walking and running so that all you have to do is to decide where to go.

(By the way, I'm going to use the term 'unconscious' throughout this. You might call it the subconscious – it's the same thing.. it's just that hypnotists have a habit of using the word 'unconscious' ambiguously to help people go into trance – we can use sneaky phrases like "because you're unconscious... mind... wants to relax")

So, can you remember when you first learnt to drive? You had to consciously think about the steering wheel, the gear shift, the mirror. Why were there three pedals when you only had two feet? What on earth do all the dials mean[2]? Everything you did you thought about consciously – which meant that getting moving was a slow, clumsy and jerky process. Fast forward a few short months, and suddenly driving has become natural. You don't think about how to use the clutch, you can now simply concentrate on working out where you are going. You've stopped doing it consciously, and now the unconscious mind has taken over running that activity for you as well.

Now the unconscious mind will carry on following the instructions it received until it receives new programming – that's instinct or habit. It's also remarkably obedient – it will accept commands and instructions from the conscious mind. The only problem is that the conscious mind is still acting as a controller – it's still acting as a controller, as a filter if you like, trying to limit what you can do and what you can change.

What's more, the unconscious mind is responsible for organising our memories. Studies seem to suggest that we actually store everything that we see. This is why police forces increasingly use hypnosis to recover information from witnesses – under hypnosis more information can be recovered. The problem seems to be that although we store everything, it's missing its index – which is why we can't recall everything. Or perhaps that's the unconscious just protecting us against this incredible mass of information – perhaps it's just presenting the information that's important at any given time.

By the way, the unconscious mind also tends to repress the negative emotions that you have – which is why you sometimes forget the unhelpful 'stuff' that has happened in your past. When the unconscious mind DOES let those memories bubble to the surface, that's because it believes that at some level you're ready

---

[2] My mother, when confronted with a rev counter for the first time, worked really hard to keep it at '30' in town – which was, of course, 3000 rpm or about 60 miles an hour. She did confess to thinking she was driving 'a wee bit fast'

to deal with them – so rejoice when that happens. It's a good thing.

The unconscious tends to take its own decisions to protect you as well – because it is responsible for your health, it sometimes takes a decision to limit you in some way to protect you from harm. Let me give you an example. When I was a kid I decided that I would go to the school fancy dress party dressed as Mercury, the Roman messenger of the gods. Everyone laughed, and so from that point on I actually became quite fearful of standing out and looking different. I started to find ways to fit in and not to be conspicuous. It wasn't until later in life that I realised what the effect of that programming had been and decided to change it. At that point in my life I realised that, actually, a messenger was exactly what I had been called to be. I reprogrammed my mind to know that standing out was a good thing. Until then though, my body's desire to protect me from emotional hurt had stopped me stepping into my destiny. Curiously, the more I explore Mercury's role, the more it fits with my role too.

So if we could find a way to get directly in touch with the unconscious mind then we would be able to release some of that unhelpful programming and **allow the body to work the way it was meant to**. Would that be useful?

This is how healing with hypnosis works, too – simply allowing the unconscious to get on and run the body properly. Many experts now believe that the only reason why the body becomes sick is because it starts producing the wrong chemicals, or not enough of the right chemicals – leading to sickness or weakening the defences so that disease can take hold. Whether that's true or not doesn't really matter – if we can give our bodies a new way of becoming healthy by working with the unconscious mind, then I don't need to know the details… I just look at the results I am getting and decide if I like them or not.

Think about it – this is exactly how a placebo drug works. A placebo is a drug given to a patient which has no biological effect – it could be a sugar pill, or chalk – something completely neutral. However, the patient is told that it's the cure – and the body starts to create the necessary immunogens or antibodies to restore the body chemistry.

So the unconscious mind is this incredibly powerful processing, thinking, creating entity that runs our bodies, takes care of us, and occasionally slips up and gets things wrong! Our goal is to learn to communicate with the unconscious directly, allowing us free access to this fabulously powerful resource.

Now, many people point to the existence of a **superconscious mind** too. Now, it doesn't matter really whether you choose to believe in this or not – why not just consider what might be possible, and then decide if you like what you achieve!

The superconscious is what connects us to each other. Essentially, say the wise ones, we are all interconnected at a deep level, and so we can actually make use of resources beyond ourselves. This is what creates the possibility of telepathy. Have you ever had a moment when you've thought about someone and a few minutes later they have called you? Have you ever had that feeling that you know what someone is thinking? That's the superconscious connecting you to 'the grid' – the network of interconnected human consciousness.

For many years spiritual leaders have been telling us that we are all one – and now, science seems to be proving that at a deep fundamental level we *are* all interconnected.

What's more, the superconscious is what connects us to the spiritual world – to the Universe, to God, to the Divine, to a power beyond ourselves - however you want to term it. So once you learn to tap into the total power of the human mind, you get connected to the power that runs the Universe. This is where the possibilities of true miracles exist. Now that's very cool indeed.

That's why meditation is so important to spiritual men and women – because it allows a direct connection between the human and the divine – **a connection to a spiritual dimension**. It does that by helping to nudge the conscious mind out of the way – allowing us to experience the superconscious directly – to have our own direct line to God.

So, if it helps you to include the superconscious in your model of the world, do so. If not, well, leave it out. Self hypnosis will still work really well for you!

Chapter 7

THE POWER INSIDE

We are living in a new era in the land of beginning again. The boundary of your dreams is the measure of your success. Dare to dream.

- Elma Easley, US entrepreneur

OK, let's look in a bit more detail how the mind works. I like to do this using the NLP communication model, simply because it helps to explain some of the keys to what's going on. If you understand what's going on in your mind, then it really helps to understand how you can make truly incredible and long lasting changes.

Tor Nørretranders suggests in the book 'The User Illusion' that we receive around 15 million bits of information every second. That's all the input from our surroundings – sight, sound, touch, taste, smell. Then our consciousness distils this down to what we are actually aware of at a conscious level. Which, when you think about it, isn't actually very much.

We may not be aware of it, but at some level **we are conscious of everything** – which is why, until I call your attention to the feeling of the chair you are sitting on, the shoe on your foot, the temperature in the room, the background sounds… you are unaware of them. Your unconscious mind is filtering out what you don't need to know about. Have you ever listened to a sound long enough that you become completely unaware of it? It just gets tuned out. That's the filtering process going on. I experienced this once when I used to work in an office above a railway station. After a while I stopped becoming aware of the station announcements below… however, at a subconscious level I had in fact memorised the entire list of stations on the Brighton to Bedford line. So while we have around 15 million pieces of information coming in, we are only really aware of 5-10 of those things at once. The truth of it, therefore, is that we don't really have a clue what's going on! We throw away so much of the information (to avoid going completely bonkers) that we can be certain that we are not in possession of all the facts at any given time.

So might that mean that you've become conditioned to certain things in your environment – things that have been around for so long that you've learnt to discount them, ignore them, pretend they don't exist? Could you, for example, be deleting some of your talents, some of your abilities? Might you be deleting some of the possibilities for your life, or the solutions to the challenges in your life?

So firstly we **delete** a huge amount of information. That's information that might be incredibly useful to us. If we can recover that information and bring it to light… well, what changes would it be possible to make?

What happens next is that we also create **generalisations** about what we experience. This allows us to make sense of different things that essentially work the same way – this is how we recognise the concept of 'chair' or 'car' without having to work out how to use every single chair or car every time we encounter one. I know that I can get into pretty much any car and have a good idea how to drive one – because I have generalised how the steering wheel, pedals, gear stick work. If I get into an automatic, I just work out the differences (and, of course, I have also generalised how 'automatic' cars work now. Generalisation is what causes us to say things like 'everyone knows that' or 'no-one can achieve that'. We affirm that 'things always go wrong for me' or 'I can never be successful'.

So might you tend group things together and miss out on the richness of life? Might you be generalising things and stopping yourself being different and standing out from the crowd? Could you be creating rules for yourself that you're afraid to break? Why not create some generalisations that actually work for you? What about affirming 'I always find it easy to learn new things' or 'I am always incredibly successful at what I attempt'?

Finally we **distort** information that we receive. We find it easy to say things like 'he doesn't trust me, otherwise he would give me more responsibility' or we look at a task and give up because it seems too complicated. These are distortions of reality.

Have you ever decided you can't do something because you're too old? Or too young? Or because you're a woman? Or because you're a man? These are distortions of reality. They're not true – but because we've held them as true for so long, we actually believe them.

We use these filters to make sense of the world – to allow us to create meaning out of what's going on. Useful as these filters are, they do not always support us effectively. The things that we distort, delete and generalise often do not serve us well. For example, 'I always get things wrong' is a generalised distortion of truth based on one or two events which has transformed itself into a belief. It's odd, though, that when we start creating these filters of reality, that actually reality tends to change to match our internal picture.

So here's a thought – if you're going to delete, distort and generalise your reality, then why not use the power of your imagination to delete, distort and generalise it in a way that supports you? Then, when reality shifts to match your internal vision, it's going to be a good thing!

The **events in our life** also shape how we perceive the world. We build filters of belief that code how we see the world. If we believe that the world is a hard, harsh, cruel, unforgiving place, then guess what we experience. If we think that everyone is a liar and a cheat – then guess what we experience. On the other hand, if we see the world as being a prosperous, friendly, abundant place and we see people as being generally good and loving, then guess what we experience instead. Now, I know what I'd prefer!

These beliefs are based on our experiences and our history. Some of them are valid, some less so. To be honest, I'd be very wary of saying any belief is 'true' – it's simply a model that you've built that supports you. Our values affect us too – if we value security and safety above all things then we will behave very differently from someone who values adventure and freedom.

Now, there's a whole load more things going on that filter our reality as well. We behave certain ways because we're programmed to (or, more accurately, because we have programmed ourselves to). That's why we might be always late for appointments, while others are always on time. That's why some of us want to plan a trip in meticulous detail while others just turn up and go for it. Some of us are happiest on our own, while others need to surround themselves with other people.

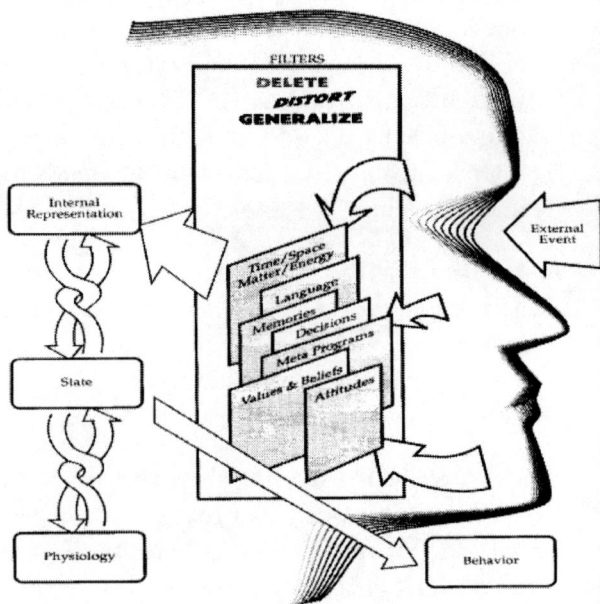

We therefore build a series of internal representations of the world, viewed through these filters. These internal representations are exactly that – they are internal to ourselves - and each person will view the same events and inputs differently based on the filters he or she is using – like "viewing the world through rose tinted spectacles' or "seeing the worst in everything' perhaps.

Think about it – this must then affect our emotions, our feelings. This must affect our confidence, our ability to feel love, our sense of freedom. This must affect how happy we feel at any given time.

Our emotions, or 'state' will then affect our actions and our behaviour. If we feel confident, then we might be ready to go on stage and make an incredible presentation, while if we don't, then we'll be afraid ever to speak in public.

Tony Robbins, the American speaker and leader, recounts the day he went to talk to singer/songwriter Carly Simon to help her with stage fright. Carly recounted that when she is backstage just before a live concert, her heart starts beating rapidly, her palms get clammy, she paces back and forth, and sweat beads on her brow. She has said that, in this moment, she just knows she can't go on stage, she's too terrified.

Later on, when Tony was talking to rock legend Bruce Springsteen, a similar story emerged. As 'The Boss' paces up and down backstage, his heart beats rapidly, his palms get clammy, sweat trickles from his hairline. But in his experience, this tells Bruce that he's "ready to rock." And he leaps onstage and has the time of his life.

Two similar experiences, two entirely different meanings. Bruce has programmed himself with a powerful meaning to his physical and emotional state – and Carly has created a completely different set of programs that don't help her at all. So here's the thing – we live life by the meanings that we attach to our experiences.

Our internal state affects two things. Firstly, it affects how we stand, how we move – our **physiology**. That's how people can tell how we're feeling. You know it, when someone's feeling sad or feeling angry, you can tell, can't you? When we're sad and nervous, then we hang our heads, breathe shallowly, move slowly. When we're happy, we stand straight, we smile and laugh, we breathe more deeply, we move more quickly. Here's the thing. Your physiology also affects your state. It's a two way street.

Try it. Think of something really sad, or maybe something you are struggling with in life. See how you are standing, feel how you are feeling. Now stand up. Really, stand up. Stand tall. Throw your head back and stretch so you're a couple of inches taller. Breathe deeply. Smile. Really, smile. Now grin. Grin wildly.

How do you feel now? Even if it's shifted you a couple of points on the happiness ladder, it's changed your emotions simply by changing how you are standing.

Our internal state also governs our **behaviour**. From how we're feeling come decisions about what we do, how we act. If we're feeling strong and powerful, we might make a decision to change our life, or to go and talk to someone new. If we feel confident we might volunteer for that new project. If we feel good about ourselves we might go and talk to that incredible person we've been eyeing up for the last half hour. If we feel confident we might believe in our own ability to become a non-smoker, or to eat healthily, or to control our compulsions, or to free ourselves from fear.

The reverse is also true – it is possible to control our state by controlling our physiology – we all know that if we smile we will feel happier, for example.

There's nothing 'wrong' with any of these programs that we run – but it's important to recognise that they are just that – programs. The beauty of this is that if we've created the program, **we can change it**.

I want you to know that you can choose to move from being 'at effect' – where you see the world as controlling you, where you do not believe you have the answer, where you believe that your situation is the result of 'circumstances' or 'other people' – to being 'at cause' – where you truly see yourself in charge of every single aspect of your life and able to create the results you truly desire. Now that's the power of self hypnosis.

So, if we want to change the RESULTS we get out of life, it makes sense that we have to change our BEHAVIOUR, doesn't it? What's more, if our behaviour is determined by our current STATE (or our emotions) then it makes sense for us to get ourselves into the best emotional state possible.

So what can we do to change our emotional state? Aren't we at the mercy of our upbringing, our environment, the events that happen around us? The short answer is… no.

In order to change our emotional state (and therefore the results we get in life) we can:

Change our physiology. Choose to stand tall. Choose to smile. Choose to behave confidently. Choose to relax.

Change our internal representation. Choose to see things as they really are. Stand back and take the overview. Get in touch with how we really feel about things. Listen to others and get objective advice.

And finally, we can *change our programming.* Truly, with the power of our unconscious minds, we can change how we've programmed ourselves, creating a new and more powerful reality.

So where does self hypnosis fit in with all this? Well, the key is in the programming. Self hypnosis allows us to work with the values, the beliefs, the filters that we have and create ones that work for us – simply by using the power of our imagination. Here's how.

First of all, we get the auditor, the conscious mind, out of the way so we can speak direct to the unconscious mind. We do this simply through relaxing the conscious mind so it lets suggestions in easily without processing or rejecting them. Because we're talking to the unconscious, then we can use lots of rich imagery and symbols, lots of pictures, anything that uses the power of the imagination. The unconscious mind loves this sort of stuff, and accepts suggestions easily.

Phew. That was quite a chapter, and quite a lot to take in. Relax. Make yourself a drink and reflect on how much power you've got... before you take the next step on your journey of exploration.

Chapter 8

BACK TO ZERO

"Cleaning helps you reduce the mortgage on your soul"

Dr Ihaleakala Hew Len, Hawaiian teacher & psychologist

LIVE WITH THE KAHUNA

Let's just take the question of our internal programs a step or two further. I've been studying the ancient Hawaiian art of Ho'oponopono for a while now. Ho'oponopono has the same spiritual heritage as Huna, probably the main belief system of Hawaii. Many people believe that much of the modern world's belief systems actually originated in Polynesia – whether that's true or not, it's worth while considering something with such a long and impressive history. In fact, Huna has a very similar approach to the conscious and unconscious mind, which is why many NLP and hypnotherapy teachers, like me, include Huna in their programmes and trainings.

The kahuna, or keepers of the secrets, believe that **we create our own reality** – in a sense that life is a waking dream, and we can choose the course of our dreams. The Australian aborigines' beliefs are very similar – for them the Dreaming was a creative place where the world was formed.

The kahuna believed that we build up memories, or programs, over time, either as we live, or by nature of being part of the human race. In Ho'oponopono, it's possible to clean the memories in order to return to the zero state or z-state. This state of being free from programming is seen as being our most God like, where **nothing exists but everything is possible.**

For students of Ho'oponopono, we clean using a simple incantation "I love you; I'm sorry; please forgive me; thank you". The very act of cleaning dissolves the toxic energy of the memory or the program.

Now, what's happening is that the negative filters and programming is being eliminated, restoring us to a state where we are clear and able to make choices for ourselves, rather than submitting to all the old 'stuff' that has dictated our paths for so long.

Think about it. If we could eliminate our internal programming, or replace it with programming that helps us, then **we would be free to write our own future, to achieve what we wanted,** free from limits and boundaries. From a position of returning to zero, erasing all negative programs, we suddenly find that anything is possible.

Now wouldn't THAT be incredible? And that is what the power of hypnosis is – to clear away all the garbage that's been clogging up your system, allowing you to have beliefs and values that truly support you, programming that serves you rather than hindering you.

SUMMING UP

So let's sum the last couple of chapters up with some more Hawaiian wisdom:

You create your own reality (ike)

You are in charge of creating your own world. Only you are going to do that. Now that might be in a purely physical, day to day, practical sense. You might set goals and taking action. You might create plans and take steps to build the reality that you want. On the other hand, you might look at this in a spiritual sense. You might create your reality through setting intentions and attracting the reality you want – through dreaming it into being.

Whatever stance you take, the truth is that you, and only you, will create the reality that surrounds you – whether it's the one you want or the one you don't want.

You get what you focus on (makia)

Whatever is the focus of our behaviour and our attention is the result that we get. Now, here's an important distinction. The unconscious mind has no concept of negatives. Think about it – if you have a child walking on a wall, and you say 'don't fall off' – the child suddenly focuses on 'falling off' and often does. Or when you're balancing plates and crockery on the way to the sink and someone says "don't drop it' – well, what's the thing we focus on? Dropping them, of course – and we often do!

So make sure that you are focussing on the right things. Focus on the positive, focus on what you are going after, not what you are moving away from. Decide what you want, and then go after that.

You are unlimited (kala)

I am certain that you have only begun to explore what you are capable of. I know that you, like me, believe that you can achieve more as you begin to learn the art of the possible – as you begin to unlock the secrets of your unconscious mind, as you begin to learn what's truly possible for someone who is connected to the Universe. As Michael Beckwith says in the movie 'The Secret':

"Are there any limits to this? Absolutely not. We are unlimited beings. We have no ceiling. The capabilities and the talents and the gifts and the power that is within every single individual that is on the planet is unlimited."

So you have a choice, don't you? You can decide to fall back into old patterns of behaviour, into old thoughts. You can choose to let the world limit you, and to believe all the old programming. Or you can choose to believe that you are incredible. Here's Michael Beckwith again:

"I believe that you're great, that there's something magnificent about you. Regardless of what has happened to you in your life. Regardless of how young or how old you think you might be. The moment you begin to think properly, this something that's within you, this power within you that's greater than the world, it will begin to emerge. It will take over your life. It will feed you. It will clothe you. It will guide you, protect you, direct you, sustain your very existence. If you let it. Now that is what I know for sure."

Chapter 9

SO WHAT'S IT LIKE?

Your vision will become clear only when you look into your heart.

- Carl Jung, Swiss psychiatrist

THE HYPNOTIC STATE

So, we have an incredibly powerful unconscious mind, capable of running our bodies perfectly. Left to its own devices, the unconscious will run the body, repairing damage and ensuring the correct balance of chemicals to keep it running at peak performance. The unconscious mind is full of imagination and doesn't really experience any limits to what's possible. The unconscious tends to behave a little like a 7-8 year old child – always looking for fun and ready to accept whatever it's told by the conscious mind. The conscious mind, on the other hand, understands its role as a responsible parent and wants to make sure the unconscious mind doesn't come to any harm. So it sets up what we call the 'critical faculty' designed to protect the unconscious from crazy suggestions. This critical faculty is what keeps us from believing what we see on TV, or keeps us sceptical when something is too good to be true.

So far so good. However, if we want to get a suggestion or new programming into the subconscious, then we have to **get the critical faculty out of the way**. When the conscious mind's back is turned, then the unconscious can accept any suggestion. So in order to dismantle the critical faculty, we relax the conscious mind – and while the conscious mind is having a well deserved snooze, or its attention is elsewhere, the suggestions and new programming get readily accepted.

BRAIN WAVES

Scientists have shown that the brain has a frequency that varies depending on what it's doing at the time. Normal awareness is called *beta* state – a frequency of above 14Hz (cycles per second). This is the frequency when you're awake, alert and doing things. When you start to relax you move into *alpha* state – a frequency of around 8-13Hz. This is the frequency of a relaxed mind – still awake, but very relaxed. After that you move into *theta* which is around 4-7Hz. This is the frequency of a very relaxed mind, or of light sleep. After that, the brain frequency goes into *delta* (0.5-3Hz) which is deep dreaming sleep – the sort of sleep that is characterised by rapid eye movement.

We're aiming to relax you to somewhere in the alpha – theta range. Believe it or not, it's actually possible to stay awake at theta and be very relaxed indeed, especially with a bit of practice.

Many people believe that sleep is the doorway to the supernormal – certainly when you lower your brainwaves to theta-delta range and stay awake (which takes practice) some very amazing things can happen!

As we'll see later, it's possible to use sound as well to help you move through these frequencies and therefore relax your mind. For example, shamans often use drums to bring people into trance like states – drums beating at rhythms in the alpha – theta ranges.

And that's it. That's all hypnosis is doing – relaxing your conscious mind so that your unconscious mind becomes far more active and accessible, ready to use its incredible power and imagination on solving problems, getting things resolved, changing your biochemistry and so on. Since our bodies and our minds are connected, then relaxing our bodies will relax our minds – so if we can relax physically, then we will relax mentally.

THE CORE STATE

OK, it's time to start on the practical side of our adventures into self hypnosis. You've learnt about the incredible power of the unconscious mind, and you've learnt how powerful you are. You've started to take responsibility for your world – your creation.

The first thing to learn is what I call the core state. This is how you want to be all the time. Wouldn't it be great if there was a way of being that allowed you to be fearless and able to make use of the incredible resources that you have open to you? Wouldn't it help you if you could remain calm, relaxed, focussed and powerful in any situation. Welcome to waking hypnosis – welcome to the power of the core state – welcome to the power of Hakalau.

Our ancient ancestors had to be far more aware of their environment than we did – largely because they needed to respond to immediate threats. They would therefore have a very wide field of view, or peripheral vision, that allowed them to be aware of movement or change in the environment. Only when a threat became apparent would they focus on that threat – and at that point the adrenalin and fight or flight reactions would kick in.

Martial artists use the same techniques. We would learn to stretch our vision around ourselves, becoming aware of things in the periphery of our vision – and even, it would feel, of things behind ourselves, things we couldn't possibly see but we seemed to be aware of. One popular karate drill is to stand in the centre of a ring of people, and any one of them can attack. The task of the karate-ka in the centre was to block the attack and launch their own counter attack. And, trust me, being whacked by a black belt isn't a 'light tap on the nose' deal, it's a 'flying across the room' thing. By maintaining awareness all around, we could sense what was going on from the slightest sound or movement.

Believe me, after getting hit a couple of times we soon learned to maintain awareness.

(I also learned to fly while doing karate…well, I went right across the room without touching the floor)

Hakalau is the Hawai'ian term for peripheral vision. With Hakalau, you remain relaxed at all times. I use Hakalau to remain calm on stage or in a meeting. In fact, I use Hakalau all the time, with the possible exception of threading a needle, when I need the focus of foveal or focussed vision!

Hakalau is a very relaxed state, and it's the state you want to be in before you go into any form of self hypnosis. In time it will become a natural state for you.

So, here's how it works.

Firstly, in every situation, BREATHE! You might laugh, but I am continually astonished how many people forget to breathe when confronted with a situation that takes them outside their comfort zone!

Deep, centred breathing brings you back to your centre, and allows you to relax even more. Slow your breathing down a little. Breathe from the diaphragm. This will mean your tummy goes out as you breathe in and fill your lungs with air right from the bottom. As you breathe out your tummy will contract. You might have learnt to breathe from your chest or even from your throat, so breathing from the stomach may not come naturally to you initially – however, the extra oxygen that it pulls in for you will soon have you feeling fabulous.

Now slow your breathing down a little more. Breathe in for a count of five, then hold it for a count of five, then breathe out for a count of five, and hold it again for a count of five. You can decide how fast you count! This is Hawai'ian **'Ha' breathing**. The kahunas would often breathe like this for hours on end, creating a deep meditative state, and referred to it as 'Touching the four corners of the Universe'.

As well as using it as relaxation for meditation, the Hawai'ians also believed that 'Ha' breathing would breathe energy into a situation, and would use 'Ha' to get situations moving, or whenever they were about to begin something new. I often do 'Ha' breathing before I go to make a presentation, or before a significant meeting.

OK, now that your breathing is nice and relaxed, let's look at your vision. I'm going to include the Hawaiian terms for these steps too.

> **Ho'ohaka:** Just pick a spot on the wall to look at, preferably about 20 degrees above your eye level. Continue to breathe deeply from the centre of your being.

> **Kuu:** "To let go." As you stare at this spot, just let your mind go loose, and focus all of your attention on the spot.

> **Lau:** "To spread out." Notice that within a matter of moments, your vision begins to spread out, and you see more in the peripheral than you do in the central part of your vision. Let your focus dissolve and relax your eyes.

> **Hakalau:** Now, pay attention to the peripheral only. Observe what's going on at the edges of your vision, without moving your eyes. Let your perception stretch right out, so that you almost become aware of what is going on behind you.

> **Ho'okohi:** "Remain." Simply stay in this state. Notice how it feels. You can drop your eyes to normal level and carry on with your life - this is a far more efficient way of being.

Have some fun with this. You might find that you start to be aware of far more than you would do otherwise. As you become better and better at it, you might even be able to sense what's behind you. You begin to pay attention to feelings, and sounds, and cues that you would not normally notice. I'm not saying that you really will be able to be aware of things that you couldn't possibly be aware of… but you might.

🔊 There's an introduction to Hakalau on the audio download – see the section on 'Further Resources'.

So, just try this out and see what happens. One thing I love to do is to use Hakalau when I am walking through a crowded shopping centre. I can be aware of exactly what's going on and just 'flow' through the crowds like the mentor and leader Morpheus does in the movie "The Matrix", striding purposefully forward as the crowds part around him, while his pupil Neo is still bumping into people.

Or try it out when you have to speak in public – or whenever you feel a bit stressed. Before you speak, just take a moment to stand still, go into the Hakalau state, and you'll find your anxieties just disappearing – and you'll find you're able to think faster and recall more of what you were going to say too.

Now, here's another thing. Hakalau is also the learning state. You'll find that you absorb far more information faster – and retain it – when you use Hakalau and peripheral vision. So next time you read, whether for pleasure or for study, go through the Hakalau drill before you start. Same for lectures – just go through the Hakalau drill as the lecture starts – and see how much more you retain. When you need to recall it, then it's easiest to just go back into the same state as when you learnt it. By the way, Hakalau or peripheral vision is the number one technique taught when you learn to speed read or photoread.

Hakalau is the cornerstone of self hypnosis, simply because it prepares the mind and relaxes you. Because it makes you more aware, you also open yourself up to the inner nudgings of your unconscious mind – and it connects you to your superconscious too.

By the way, you'll have noticed that Hakalau is something you can do *with your eyes open*. So that opens up the possibility of being in a state of self hypnosis with your eyes open, doesn't it?! Now, it might be better, if you're going to relax, to shut your eyes as you would when you sleep, which also helps get rid of all the distractions… but it's not essential. You're going to find as you read this manual (which I'm guessing you are going to do with your eyes open) that you might find yourself in a bit of a trance here and there. So while I'd recommend that you have eyes closed… it's not essential, and it's OK if you want to keep them open too.

YOUR IMAGINATION

Now that you've had a chance to experience the core state for self hypnosis, let's actually experience hypnosis itself for the first time. Well, actually, it won't be for the first time at all. Being in a trance is a really natural, normal, waking state. You've been in trance many times. You've been in trance when you're watching the TV or a movie – you're relaxed, your imagination is working, and you're transported into another world. You're in trance. Ever driven on a familiar route and found yourself arriving at your destination with no conscious recollection of driving the route? You're in trance. Ever got really caught up in a good book, so you can almost see the action going on? You're in trance.

So it really is a normal, natural state of being, a feeling of being relaxed and at peace. You might feel your brain fizzing a bit when you're in trance, you might not. You might feel a little limp, you might not. Incredibly, as I've said, you can be in trance even with your eyes open. It is, however, a really pleasant, really relaxed, peaceful, calm, tranquil state for both your mind and your body.

It's not like being asleep – you remain aware of what's going on, but you just feel SO relaxed that nothing really matters. If you drift off to sleep then that's OK (although that's technically called 'sleeping' not 'self hypnosis'!), but it's normal to just stay aware of what's going on and almost observe what's going on with perhaps an amused detachment.

So, you're going to be aware of what's going on at all times, and you're going to be completely in control of what's going on too.

With self hypnosis, the question of being 'controlled' doesn't really come up, but it's worth while mentioning it now. The truth of the matter is that all hypnosis is self hypnosis, so you remain in control. It's you that chooses to go into a trance, and it's you that chooses what you do when you are in a trance. All that a hypnotist can do is to work with your desires and your dreams and goals to help you achieve what you want. We have some cool techniques to help you relax and go into trance, and we have some great skills in constructing suggestions that help you change your life, but in the end, *you* choose to go into hypnosis.

Even when you see a stage hypnosis show, where people are imitating Elvis or playing out scenes from 'The Full Monty' you will still find that those people feel completely in control and are aware of everything that goes on. And, yes, I have seen those XXX hypnosis shows too, where anything goes... and all that's happening is that the participants have been prepared to suspend reality for a while (and, yes, I'm sure, act out some of their inner fantasies!)

So, you're going to remain in control at all times, OK?!

A friend of mine has been practicing self hypnosis for years: in fact she uses it instead of local anaesthetic at the doctors or dentists. She put it really well when she said that when she goes into a trance state it's almost like flipping a switch. It's like switching the brain off so that thought itself almost stops. There's no analysis going on, no logic, no thinking – just your imagination, and anything's possible. It's as if your conscious mind just drains out of you, so that nothing matters in that moment, and it's all OK. You'll find that you're almost a detached observer[3] of what's going on.

JUST IMAGINE....

Let's just try a little test of the imagination. So sit yourself somewhere comfortable, and relax....I want you to really get in touch with the next few paragraphs and let your imagination go... read nice and slowly ....and really let yourself be drawn into the story...

◀€ I want you to imagine yourself walking into your kitchen, or the kitchen of someone you know. It's a beautiful sunny day, and the sunlight is streaming through the kitchen windows, and you can just see the little particles of dust in the air. The kitchen feels comfortably warm, heated by the gentle sunshine. By contrast, the floor feels cool and smooth under your feet. You decide that you'd like a drink, so you walk over to the refrigerator and pull the door open. The seal on the door resists slightly and then the door swings open easily. You hear the sound of the seal separating, and a draft of cool air wafts over your arm and the refrigerator light goes on. You look into the refrigerator, and in amongst the food and drink, the fruit and vegetables, you see a beautiful bowl at the bottom of the refrigerator. It's a blue and white striped bowl, and in the bowl lie several plump, juicy lemons. You select the juiciest, plumpest, ripest lemon from the bowl, and shut the refrigerator door, the seal just pulling the door shut as you close it.

---

[3] Advanced brain researchers and researchers in quantum physics point to there being 'an observer' function in each of us who seems to be separate from the brain and consciousness functions. So it really does seem as if the mind 'switches off' leaving an observer to watch what's going on. Follow that rabbit hole further and you'll find that maybe, just maybe, that it's that observer that creates our individual reality. Now that's 'spooky stuff'.

You feel the waxy skin of the lemon in your hand, smooth and yet bumpy at the same time, and you can just smell the faint scent of lemon zest as you walk over to the worktop counter. You take a knife from the drawer and put the lemon down on the counter. Carefully you cut the lemon in half, and you hear the 'tsss' sound of the lemon zest while the juice squirts out over your fingers. You can smell the crisp, clear lemon scent even more now, and you can almost taste the lemon on your tongue. You pick half of the lemon up and look at the rind, the pith, and the seeds of the lemon, nestling amongst the juicy centre of the lemon. Just give that lemon a gentle squeeze, and as the scent of the lemon increases, some of the juice runs slowly down your hand.

Now take that lemon up to your nose and breathe in that sharp, tangy lemony scent. Now open your mouth and take a huge bit of the lemon. The juice squirts out of the lemon and runs down your chin, and you feel the incredibly tart and bitter juices of the lemon on your tongue.

Now, what did you experience? Most people will feel an increase in saliva. Many people will pull a face as they experience the sourness of the lemon. Even those few who don't experience anything will realise that they knew what was happening and were actively resisting using their imaginations.

So, just to make sure you're aware... there was no refrigerator. There was no lemon. It was all in your imagination, and your imagination, being hard wired to your body, produced a chemical reaction. Hypnosis works exactly the same way – by relaxing and using your imagination, you can change what's happening in your body.. for example, you can use hypnosis to help you give up smoking... dissolve eating disorders... lose weight... build confidence... relax...

In fact, I think the applications of hypnosis are limited only by your imagination... so since your imagination is unlimited, then you are about to experience an unlimited opportunity to get the results you want in your life. Are you ready?

SAFETY FIRST

I just wanted to say a few words about the dangers of self hypnosis – and I realised that there weren't any, really. We know that all hypnosis is self hypnosis anyway, so there's no way that anyone can convince you to do something you don't want to – so how you yourself could convince yourself to do something that you don't want to, I don't really know. Actually, it makes my head hurt to think about it.

So here's a few thoughts to **put your mind at rest**...

You can't hypnotise yourself so deeply that you can't come back. You might drift off for a snooze, but you'll awaken naturally anyway. If you're worried about snoozing for too long, then set an alarm. You don't want to go for a quick energizer break at work and drift off for so long the boss notices, do you? (By the way, the body has a useful alarm function installed to help you wake up from sleep – it's called 'the bladder'.)

You shouldn't be using self hypnosis programmes while you're driving a car or operating machinery. I'd avoid subliminal CDs or hypnosis CDs in this situation. I'd also avoid using self hypnosis to relax you when you're driving. It just makes sense. Also, when you come back out of a hypnotic state, just take a few moments to come fully awake. In fact, when I'm driving for long periods, I often use self hypnosis to take a quick break from driving – I pull off the road, turn the ignition off, go into a brief trance and then I'm refreshed and ready to go... but I *always* make sure I'm fully awake before driving off!

No-one is going to be able to take advantage of your hypnotic state against your will. Remember, you're going to be aware of what's going on, and it's YOUR hypnosis session, OK?

I just wanted to make sure that any of you who are real 'control' people out there are relaxed about hypnosis. Some people don't find it easy to just let go – they want to know what's going on at all times. Now with self hypnosis, of course, there's only going to be you running the show, so that's OK – but even so, it's not always easy to just let go. Here's the thing to remember: you are more than your brain and your mind. You can just stop 'thinking' and just observe, with detached amusement, what's going on. Any time you want you can start your brain up again... but just for a while imagine what it would be like without really thinking...

Chapter 10

YOU'RE FEELING SLEEPY....

"Man can learn nothing except by going from the known to the unknown."

- Claude Bernard, French physiologist

SO WHAT'S GOING ON?

OK, we've looked at the basics and the 'core state', and you've had an experience of using your imagination... so I think you're ready to learn the hypnotic process for yourself, don't you?

Now, here's the one thing that I want you to remember. HAVE FUN! **Enjoy this.** Look on it as a game – that way you're going to enjoy the learning process, and your inner child or unconscious mind is going to want to come out and play. Explore. See what happens. There's no right or wrong answer – just an experience.

So before we actually get into experiencing hypnosis, I just wanted to help you understand the process of hypnosis and how it's going to work for self hypnosis. It's just the same, by the way: the only thing that's different when you go to a hypnotherapist is that you get someone to facilitate and assist you.

There are typically 7 steps to a great hypnosis session – we'll go into these in some detail in a moment.

Preparation – checking your environment and your purpose

Getting ready – making yourself comfortable & relaxing yourself.

Induction – your hypnotic induction into trance.

Deepening – techniques to help you deepen your trance.

Convincers – how to know if you are in trance

Suggestions – where you give yourself the programming for the results you want.

Coming back – returning back to full consciousness

Let's go through each of these stages in a bit more detail:

Preparation

First of all, **check your environment**. If you are going to relax, then you want to make sure that you are in a relaxing environment. That makes sense, surely? So, try and make sure that you've got a great environment available to you. I'll talk about a few ways you can make it even better later, but for the moment just concentrate on the following:

☐ Get a comfortable chair – not too relaxing, as you don't want to go to sleep (and best not doing self hypnosis lying down - unless you DO want to go to sleep, in which case, go right ahead, be my guest!)

☐ Find a nice peaceful place where you won't be disturbed. Nowadays you can't avoid all background noise, but just know that any sounds you hear are simply going to help you go even deeper into trance.

☐ If you can, make sure that the temperature is comfortable. Too warm and you're going to become too sleepy, while too cold or draughty and you're going to find it difficult to relax, especially if you start shivering!

☐ If you want, set a timer for the end of your session.. or just come back when you're ready. If you need to be finished at a particular time, then having a timer helps you relax knowing you will be reminded of the time.

Then **determine your goals**. What are you looking to achieve through this hypnosis session? Look at the section on Getting Results to make sure you're clear about what you're doing and why. You might choose to write them out, or you might choose to embed them in your memory (so that you can do it with your eyes closed!). What suggestions are you going to give yourself? What do you want to explore? What do you want to change in your body chemistry? Are you looking to connect with the Divine as a meditation process? Even if you're just taking a time out to relax or to rest, why not give yourself a suggestion such as "When I wake I will feel refreshed and enthusiastic, ready to step up and pursue my life". Or whatever works for you.

Make sure you've got your intention clear in your conscious mind, and then it will simply sink down into your unconscious mind as you go deep into trance.

Getting ready

OK, sit back and **relax..**

Sit down in your chair and make yourself nice and comfortable. Put your feet flat on the floor, and rest your hands gently in your lap or on your knees. Take a nice, deep refreshing breath – and then another deep, relaxing, comfortable breath. Now find a spot on the wall above your line of sight and focus on that spot. Let your awareness stretch all around yourself as you relax your vision using the Hakalau core hypnotic state, until you can almost become aware of what is going on behind you. Now you can close your eyes and relax....

Induction

This is the core part of the hypnosis process. We'll cover a full induction in the next chapter, but the goal is to relax you more and more. For self hypnosis this is usually done using 'tense and relax' where you tense your muscles and then relax them progressively across your body. I also use one or two visualisations to help myself relax further.

Deepening

Deepening techniques just help you increase the level of trance. You don't need to use these, but they are quite useful to produce a deeper level of trance. Again, we'll look in detail at these in a future chapter, but some ways of deepening trance include counting numbers down, or descending a flight of steps, or letting numbers disappear from a whiteboard.

Convincers

So, am I hypnotised? Well, here's the thing. Do you feel relaxed? Do you feel calm? Hypnosis is a very personal thing, but some ways of telling if you're in trance follow... and you might find others. Some people feel completely limp and relaxed, like a damp dishrag. You might like to try and open your eyes, and find, with some amusement, that you cannot. You might feel a fizzing in your scalp or your brain. You might find that, try as you may, you cannot move your arms, or perhaps your legs feel like lead.

One of my earliest memories of a hypnotic state was when I was about 11 or 12 and one of my friends was reading me a story. As she read to me I could feel a real tingling in my mind. I could have stayed there and listened to her for ever.

And of course, you might just decide 'I must be in a trance'. Why not?

Suggestions

This is where you insert your goals for the session. As I say, these might be suggestions to your body to heal, or to help you reprogram your consciousness. It might be a request to find answers to a particular problem, or it might be a simple meditation.

Coming back

A typical hypnotist will count their client back out of a trance. You can do exactly the same thing, just count back from 1 to 10 and become more awake with each number you count. If you want to set an alarm, then that might well waken you quickly. Just take time to come round fully before rushing off!

If you've been looking for insights then it's worth recording any experience that you've had, any answers you got, any truths that came to you.

So now you know all that, then it's time… to **go into trance**

Chapter 11

DRIFTING, DROPPING, DREAMING, FALLING

"Dreams don't come true. They are true."

- Tom Robbins (US Novelist)

You've read this far through this manual, and that means that you're ready to go into trance…

SO JUST RELAX.. THAT'S RIGHT.. VERY GOOD..

What I am going to do is to give you a script to follow. Then when you do this on your own you'll know what to do and you've got a basis for what works for you. You don't need to read this out, just follow along. I'd suggest that you read through this section a couple of times, and then try it for yourself with your eyes open. Even with your eyes open you're going to find yourself going into a relaxed state as you tense and then relax each part of your body.

Then try again with your eyes closed. And relax – there's no 'right way' so whatever you do is going to be fine. You'll probably find this section a bit hypnotic.. and that's fine.

Here goes then – enjoy your trip…

◀ So, find a nice peaceful spot and make yourself comfortable. Let all the distractions just recede into the background, just let them go, you don't need to even have them in your consciousness right now. Just let them disappear from your mind… if you need them later you can pick them up if they are still important, but for right now, just let them go...

Any sounds that you hear are just indicators that you are going even deeper into trance, and becoming even more relaxed.

And if any thoughts should come up, you can feel free to just let those thoughts go too... it's OK, just let them drift off into the distance, you can pick them up later if you need to but for now just let them drift away like clouds in the sky.

Now breathe deeply, a nice deep relaxing breath... Take your time over this wonderful, easy, simple breath. Breathe in for a count of five... then breathe out for a count of five... and as you breathe out, just let anything that is still in your awareness just drift away. That's right. Take about ten deep, refreshing, relaxing, calming breaths, and you will find yourself truly connected to the world, and the Earth, and the Universe... you will feel steady, stable, grounded, at peace....

And breathe again, another deep, relaxing, calm beautiful breath... Feel the oxygen come into your body, and make its way to your brain.

Now just find a spot on the wall just above your line of vision. As you focus on that spot, just let your vision relax and become a little unfocussed.... Let your vision spread out a little, so you become aware of even more of the room, and in this wonderful relaxed state, let your awareness spread out and around you, becoming more aware of the room now, letting your awareness stretch out to the side, so you become aware of more objects that you could see before... and almost being able to sense what's going on behind you now.

And now you can simply close your eyes [although right now that's going to make reading the rest of this chapter tricky!]. Just let the temperature in the room support you in going into trance and helping you become even more relaxed....

Now I just going to ask you to tense and relax different parts of your body... First of all, simply tense the muscles in your feet, and your ankles - curl your toes up and tense... tense... and relax now, letting that relaxation flood through your feet and to your ankles... now tense your leg muscles... tense... tense... and now just relax and let that relaxation spread all the way from your thighs down to your calves, leaving your legs feeling totally relaxed, so relaxed that you don't know if you can move your legs at all... and it's OK, because you don't even want to try.

> [This works even better if you lift your legs off the ground as you tense them – then as you let go just let your legs drop, feeling limp and relaxed, like a dishrag, just let all the tension drain out]

Now tense your chest, and your abdomen... tense... tense... and relax now, letting a beautiful warm feeling of relaxation flood through your torso from deep in your stomach, just flowing gently out, warming you from the inside out...

And now you can simply just tense your hands... tense... tense... and relax them now, just let that feeling of relaxation flow over your hands, feeling good to be so relaxed. Now tense your arms and your shoulders... tense... tense... and relax them now, feeling that feeling of wonderful deep relaxation flow from your shoulders, down your upper arms, around your elbows and your forearms and into your wrists.

> [Again, this works best if you actually hold your arms palms up and lift your arms off your lap as you tense them, and then just let the arm plop back into your lap, palms down and limp as a dishcloth, as you release the tension. You'll probably find as you tense your arms that your shoulders rise and hunch a little.. so just let those shoulders drop and let all the tension whoosh out of your body]

And now tense all the muscles in your face... your jaw... your eyes and the muscles around your eyes... just direct your attention to the muscles round your eyes for a moment, and tense... tense... and then just let it all go, just let yourself relax... let your head go limp.

Now we're going to put it all together... tense your arms, your hands, your shoulders, your legs, your body, your head, your jaw, your eyes.... And just hold that moment of tension.... And hold it again.... And hold it.... And then just let go... let it all go and just relax....let that feeling of relaxation just wash up and down your body. It feels so good...just let yourself go limp and relax every muscle in your body.

> [At this point, you want to tense your entire body as hard as you can. It works even better if you actually lift your arms off your lap and lift your legs off the floor and then let them drop. Hold that tension, carry on holding it and suddenly let go of all the tension you've held in, almost in a big 'whoosh' feeling. Let your body really sag and go limp as if all the muscles have stopped working]

I'd like you to just imagine a beautiful beam of white light shining down on the top of your head... Just enjoy that beautiful feeling of light shining down on you, warming you slightly... Let that feeling of radiance just drift gently over the rest of your body, enveloping you in a warm cloak of loving energy... Enjoy the feeling of warmth as it reaches over your entire body feel the warmth and surge of calm, hypnotic, relaxing energy... and you might find a tingling fizzing sensation moving across the top of your head as you let that energy just drift across your mind... Let that feeling of hypnotic calm just relax each and every one of your muscles... it feels so good, doesn't it, so relaxing, so easy...just enjoy that moment of total relaxation....

OK, that's the hypnotic induction. When you try this you're going to feel really, really relaxed, and that's great. In the next chapter we're going to learn a few tips and techniques for helping you go deeper and deeper into trance. However, why don't you just read through this set of instructions a couple of times, then read through it and actually DO the tensing exercises as you read – then finally try it for yourself with your eyes closed and see how good it feels.

You can do this in bed, by the way, it really helps you to drift off to sleep (it's the same principle as drifting off to sleep after sex.. the sudden relaxation and release just sends you off to the land of nod). I used to do this exercise on airplanes too – they're notoriously difficult to get to sleep on.

Chapter 12

AM I IN A TRANCE?

"First we have a question; then dreams, daydreams, and intuitions lead us towards the answers"

- James Redfield, The Celestine Prophecies

OK, so we've looked at a basic induction. That will get you nicely into a trance state. You might at this point be wondering "am I hypnotized?" Well, here's how you know. If you want to be – you are! As I said earlier, going into a trance is a natural, normal, easy thing that you do every day. **You're good at it**.

You probably want to create a deeper level of trance, and that's where the deepening techniques we're going to look at will help you.. after then you can ask yourself the question again and know that you're in a trance.

GOING DEEPER

Now, the basic induction in the previous chapter is going to work just fine. What's more, each time you do it you're going to find it easier and easier – this is a process called fractionation – each time you go into trance and then come back out it's a little bit easier to go a little bit deeper each time. So you just need to practice a bit and **you'll find your level of trance improve** each time.

If you do at any time find your mind wandering away, that's fine. Just notice the fact that it's wandering away. You can choose to bring it back if you wish... or not... it's entirely up to you. If you're just relaxing, then let your mind skitter off and do what it wants. If you're pursuing a specific goal you might want to let it come back so you keep on track.

However, if you want to get to deeper and deeper levels then here are some great deepening ideas. Use one, use them all, it doesn't matter. The key, at all times, is to do *what works for you*.

First, try simply repeating to yourself '**Drifting, dropping, dreaming, falling**' over and over again. This simple little mantra really helps the feeling of just drifting away into a wonderful sleep.

You can consciously monitor and slow the rate of your breathing down even more... breathe nice and shallowly now, but just slow you breath down bit by bit, although you don't need to focus on your breathing, just let it go... nice and easy...

Another option I really like is to imagine a yard stick or a stick with numbers on, or maybe a series of numbers stretching out into the distance. Just count the numbers down and decide that when you reach (say) 5 then you'll be in a deep state of hypnotic trance. "36... 35... 34... 33..." and so on. Match the pace of the number with your breathing and say the number to yourself in your mind on your outbreath.

> Drifting, dropping, dreaming, falling... deeper and deeper.

Many people like to imagine a classroom blackboard or whiteboard with number on it. Just slowly erase each of the numbers one by one, wipe them off, it doesn't matter, you know that you can get them back any time you want to, but for now, just let them go, it's OK.

If it works better for you, then imagine the whiteboard is filled with writing, or perhaps a complicated science formula (go on, you know you hated those at school) and you can just imagine that being erased bit by bit... it doesn't matter, does it? Or imagine that you're reading a book, and the letters just drip off the edge of the page, sliding to the bottom of the page and letting them go….

> Drifting, dropping, dreaming, falling… deeper and deeper.

A friend of mine just imagines every bit of her consciousness draining out of her – it's ok, it doesn't matter, and she lets the energy and awareness just leave her body – if you try it now you can just feel the energy draining from you as you relax more and more..

> Drifting, dropping, dreaming, falling… deeper and deeper.

One thing that I often do, and have done since I was quite small, is to tell a story to myself. It doesn't matter what story you tell, as long as it's going to relax you.

🔈 Maybe you're walking along a wonderful, peaceful beach, enjoying a wonderful warm, sunny day, with the sound of the waves breaking gently on the shoreline. You can hear the whisper of the leaves in the trees, and in the distance the tropical sound of cicadas in the leaves. The sun is just setting, and a beautiful orange glow spreads across the skyline as the most beautiful sunset you have ever see lights up the evening sky. You come to a little stream, burbling and babbling as it finds its way down to the sea. You decide that you're going to follow the stream as it leads inland, and as you follow the stream you come to a set of ten beautiful stone steps, with little lights by the side to guide your way down. You decide to follow these beautiful steps, and you step slowly down each one. By the side of the steps are beautiful flowers, and the gorgeous scent of the flowers just wafts about you dreamily as you slowly step down one by one. 10... 9... 8... 7... 6... 5... 4... 3... 2... 1... last step now... at the bottom now, you see a beautiful mossy stone, worn smooth by the people who have rested on it before... so you decide to simply spend a few moments resting by that beautiful rock and enjoying a few minutes of well earned rest and relaxation in that beautiful grove, warmed by the summer sun and so, so peaceful..

You get the idea. Again, you make up your own story. Give your imagination plenty to work on. If you prefer a walk in the woods, rather than the beach, then that works well. If you're a snow sort of person, like I am, then go for a walk in the snow. Or you could imagine yourself skiing calmly and confidently down a mountain side – and you can use the schusses of the rhythmic turns to relax you and create a rhythm to take you deeper and deeper. If you can include any elements of going down, or drifting, then that works really well.

A great alternative is to imagine yourself getting into an elevator, and feeling it whisking you down deeper and deeper underground. As you experience the feeling of dropping that you get in an elevator, that 'whoosh' feeling will drop you further and further into a hypnotic state. You can count the floors from 10 to zero, or from zero to 10, or whatever way works for you.

When you want to come back from your hypnotic trance then you can just reverse the story (or count yourself back, it doesn't matter)

(Now, while I think about it, a quick word on counting into trance. Some people prefer to enter trance counting from 10 to 1, others like to count from 1 to 10. It doesn't really matter too much. I like to use 10 to 1 because then there is a really defined end point at which I know I am going to be in trance (and I can use a really hypnotic zzerroooo… at the end when I'm working with someone). I also like the fact that I am counting *down* as we seem to go 'down' into trance.

Others like to count up, because that way there's no end to how far you can count, and bigger numbers are a bit more trancy and hard to grasp.

This is self hypnosis – do what works for you. When you count yourself back out of trance, simply reverse the sequence.

AM I HYPNOTIZED?

OK, so far so good. You've taken yourself through a hypnotic induction, and you've let that trance deepen. One of the things about hypnosis, and self hypnosis in particular, is that you can find yourself asking the perfectly reasonable question "did it work?" So how can you convince yourself that you're hypnotised?

Well, here's a couple of things you might well experience:

You might find your scalp or your brain feeling a little bit 'fizzy'. It's a strange but very pleasant experience, almost as if there's a little electrical energy current running round your head. You might even find that stretches down your spine, or into your arms or the rest of your body.

You will almost certainly feel very very relaxed. Your arms will feel leaden, and your legs just aren't going to want to move at all. In fact, you will probably be asking yourself "why bother moving at all".

You might like to put your attention on your eyelids, and allow those eyes to become even more relaxed, and even more and as you do they become even more heavy. You only need to try to open them when you are sure you cannot. You find that even though you might try to open them, that you cannot, they are too tired, it's so wonderful staying in this trance, you just can't be bothered to even try to open them. And as you relax your eyes now you find yourself becoming even more drowsy, even more at peace, even more relaxed. Drifting, dropping, dreaming, falling… deeper and deeper.

(By the way, as Yoda said in Star Wars: "Do, or do not, there is no 'try'" – you can't 'try' to do anything. Try and pick up a pencil. Go on, really try. Did you succeed? If so, then you weren't trying – you were succeeding. Did you fail? If so, then you weren't trying, were you?)

Or you might put your attention on your legs, and enjoy that feeling of relaxation as it moves down your legs, to the point where you simply do not want to be bothered to even try to lift your legs. Only try to move your legs when you are sure you cannot, and enjoy that feeling of heaviness in your legs... so relaxed... so peaceful. It doesn't matter, does it... so just let your legs relax even more, and as you do you will go even deeper into a wonderful, comfortable, refreshing trance. Drifting, dropping, dreaming, falling... deeper and deeper.

It's perfectly normal for your brain to be running around thinking "am I hypnotised?" and in fact it's a good thing. You see, while the brain is occupied in this way, the suggestions can go deep into your unconscious mind. Your conscious mind is away worrying about whether you're hypnotised or not, so your unconscious can just take advantage of that.

If you're worried that you might be faking being hypnotised, then that's OK too. Why not just pretend that you're hypnotised, and then pretend that you're not pretending any more (you might laugh, but at this level of working with your unconscious, that actually makes sense – at least to your unconscious mind!)

By the way, now you're here, it's worth just creating a suggestion that it will be easy to go back this place next time. You might like to say something like "and when I visualise this place, and as I say the words "Relax" and visualise the number zero I will find myself coming back easily and naturally to this place". As you repeat the experience it will become easier and easier to relax, to the point that you don't need to go through the induction, you can just step immediately to this place (and then, if you want to , you can relax yourself even more)

COMING BACK TO EARTH

Getting back out of trance is easy. Just decide you want to come back. (I told you it was easy). If you have a specific time that you need to be awake by, then consider setting a timer, although I'd prefer something quiet or with a crescendo alarm that starts off quiet. Having a timer will help if you're feeling a bit worried that you might drift off – so if it lets you relax it's a good thing. To be honest, in self hypnosis you're going to remain conscious – if you get really relaxed or you are very tired then you might drift off to sleep, so then an alarm might be the easiest.

You can count yourself out of the trance, something like

1.. becoming more awake now.. 2.. moving fingers and toes.. 3.. feeling the feelings returning to your body.. 4.. just moving arms and legs, feeling full of energy.. 5.. feeling wide awake and refreshed, ready to face the day.

You don't need to count out to the same number as you counted in, by the way, just know that when you reach the end of your count you will be wide awake. Of course, if you want to then that's OK too. It's a good idea, though, to count in the opposite direction to the one you use when entering trance.

So, if you enter trance by counting down from 10 to 1 then when you come back up, count from 1 to 5, or 1 to 10. Just reverse the direction.

Chapter 13

PUTTING IT TOGETHER

"When man is dreaming, he is a genius"

— Akira Kurosawa, Japanese film director

OK, so let's put all that together and see how it flows. What I've done is to give you the whole script without any commentary in the Further Resources section 'The Full Script', so you can use that on your own. In the section 'Continuing the Adventure', I've also given details of how to get a copy of the induction on audio so you can listen along. Sometimes that makes it easier, particularly when you're learning this stuff. As you get more experienced, you can drop the script and the audio and just do it yourself.

So here are the steps

1. Make sure you have a nice comfortable environment

    - quiet and undisturbed

    - with a comfy chair

2. Set your intention or your goal for the session

    - goal setting

    - meditation

    - dealing with issues

    - sitting for ideas

3. Get yourself ready

    - simply relax and get comfortable

    - take a few nice deep relaxing breaths

    - relax your vision with Hakalau

    - close your eyes

    - breathe deeply 10 times or so

4. Induction

    - Tense & relax your feet

    - Tense & relax your legs (lift & drop)

    - Tense & relax your body

    - Tense & relax your arms & shoulders (lift & drop)

    - Tense & relax your head

    - Tense & relax your whole body (lift & drop)

    - Drifting, dropping, dreaming, falling…..

5. Deepen the trance

    - Counting numbers into the distance

    - Counting down a yardstick

    - Let numbers disappear from a whiteboard

    - Story

6. Convince yourself

    - How are you feeling? Relaxed? Good!

    - Try (and only try) to lift your legs

- Try (and only try) to open your eyes

- Pretend you're hypnotised

7. Go through your intention for the session

8. Bring yourself back

- count yourself back

- walk back through your story

- preserve any lessons from the experience

And that's it. Easy.

Now, you're might not be perfect first time out (hold on a second – what is perfect for this anyway? Just **do what works**, what relaxes you, what you enjoy.) There is no right or wrong way: the goal is simply to get you to a new level of conscious relaxation. That's it.

Now that you're nicely relaxed, I suggest that you set a trigger that will take you nicely and easily back into trance. It might be that you say to yourself 'Relax' in a nice deep hypnotic voice. Or you might visualise something – when you visualise a particular scene for example. You might like to use a simple touch, perhaps the inside of your wrist (don't go for somewhere someone might touch you normally – you don't want to just collapse when someone touches your hand now, do you?!

You could even see a switch in your mind and just let that switch trigger the trance state – just breathe and then flick the switch – out like a light! As you get to be really good at this, then you really can just go 'out like a light' in demand as you go into trance. You'll find there's a really clear difference between 'awake' and 'trance' as you just flick the metaphorical switch and go within yourself, becoming a detached observer of what's going on as your mind just seems to shut down. And that's OK, by the way.

The key to setting these triggers is to get yourself into trance, think of the picture you want, or make the gesture you want, and your mind will link the trigger to the state you're in. In NLP this is called anchoring, as we are anchoring a state of 'being' to a trigger from one of our senses. You're making a two way link: if a particular state is linked to a specific trigger, then the specific trigger is linked to the specific state…. and means that when you fire the trigger, you get the state back.

These triggers will help you go back into trance – your neurology will link up the trigger with the state that you're in, make the association and then you'll be able to repeat it on demand. You'll probably want to go through some part of the induction/deepening process, but it will make it so much easier to go even deeper next time round.

Try it out, practice, try it different ways. Have a go and enjoy the experience – have fun with this.

Chapter 14

SOME IDEAS TO HELP YOU

Take the first step, and your mind will mobilize all its forces to your aid. But the first essential is that you begin. Once the battle is startled, all that is within and without you will come to your assistance

- Robert Collier, US Author

It's perfectly simple to go into trance on your own, any time. I use it to get to sleep on aeroplanes (when I'm a passenger, not when I'm flying!), or any time I need a quick energy boost. I will often go into a light trance just to get insight into a problem. Sometimes, though, it can help you to have some extra tricks up your sleeve, just to make things a little bit special, or just to help you get into trance more quickly.

THE SOUND OF MUSIC

Firstly, music. Music can really help you relax, as your ears are soothed by the music while your heart rate and thought frequencies will automatically synchronise with the music. We all have very positive associations to music as a way of changing our state – we have fast, bouncy tracks with lots of rhythm for dancing that make us feel great at parties. We have music that inspires us and fills our hearts with joy, and music that makes us cry every time we hear it.

It's the same with relaxation. We can use music to gently relax us, leading us into trance. We also have great associations with music when our parents used to sing us lullabies to relax us and send us off to sleep when we were little.

When selecting music to use, simply find something that you like, and that relaxes you. Browse in a new age bookshop, or listen to a few tracks on line. I've listed one or two great sites where you can get relaxation music in the 'Continuing the Adventure' section. One of my friends, Dr Topher Morrison (who was also the guy who taught me hypnosis) has two CDs of relaxation music that are based on the rhythms of nursery rhymes. They are very cool indeed. The only guidelines I would suggest when choosing your music is to make sure that there are no sudden tempo changes, or crescendos as this can interrupt your relaxation. I'd also avoid anything with a solo vocal track, although choirs work quite well for many people. I also personally like to have music with more bass as this tends to resonate with the body. Experiment, ask around, and have fun.

Another thing that people like are ambient soundtracks. These are things like recordings of the sea gently washing on the shore, or a gentle tropical rainstorm. Other people like the sounds of a forest or a gently babbling brook, or the sound of crickets and cicadas on a hot tropical evening. I am particularly fond of a recording I have of a summer thunderstorm – I can feel the connection to power in the rumble of thunder.

Again, experiment to see what you like – or what reminds you of a particularly peaceful experience in your life.

While we're discussing water, you can now buy little indoor fountains. The gentle gurgle of these decorations really do help to soothe and relax – although if you're fortunate enough to have a fountain in your garden, feel free to use that, of course! The additional benefit of a fountain is that it releases negative ions into the atmosphere, which can be very 'clearing' and creates very fresh air. Another way of doing that is to buy an ionizer, which has the same effect. Of course, if you have the budget, buy a mountain stream. All joking aside, though, try taking a walk in nature or by the beach, and experience the natural sounds of water running over rocks or washing up the sand, and see how relaxing it is. And why not sit and listen to a rainstorm – this is my all time favourite way of getting new insights – I've been known to drop everything I'm doing, put my coat on and go outside when it starts to rain.

SWING TO THE BEAT

You can also obtain 'click tracks' that are designed to lower your brain frequency. Remember we talked earlier about alpha and theta brainwaves? Click tracks are designed to simply lower your brain frequency from its normal beta frequency to either alpha (chilled and relaxed) or theta (the level of sleep). Check out the 'Continuing the Adventure' section for how to get hold of these tracks to help you.

One of my friends reminded me of the relaxing effect of swinging, whether it's a playground swing or a luxury hammock: again, it tends to lower the brain frequencies (remember the old staple of movie hypnotists – the swinging pocket watch?). I think the swinging balls of the Newton's cradle have a very similar effect, and the clicks work well to slow your brain waves down (you want a larger model for this as the swings are slower) – I've always found this to be very hypnotic. So a rocking chair might work well for you.

Some people like to have something to do with their hands as they meditate or do self hypnosis. Rosary beads work quite well, or Chinese meditation balls that chime gently as you turn them in your hand. If your purpose is meditation then this could work really well for you.

SENSUAL HYPNOSIS

You might like to burn some incense or a scented candle – this is particularly great for meditation. Same goes for aromatherapy burners. The sense of smell completely bypasses the hypothalamus, going straight to the brain, so if you have some scents and smells that relax you, then they will have a particularly potent effect. I'd suggest that you use these particular scents only for your self hypnosis or meditation sessions – if you have them around the house all day then the effect will lessen as you get used to them. The act of lighting the incense also becomes a great ritual that will help you getting ready for your session.

You can also use aromatherapy tubes for this – they are particularly useful for carrying in your pocket.

We also tend to associate warmth with relaxation, so make sure you are at a comfortable temperature. Of course, if you are too warm you might fall asleep, but I've personally found that shivering and goosebumps don't help me relax!

One little tip that I have found really helpful is to just gently massage or stroke your head before you start – just let the tips of your fingers drift through your hair (not that I know how that feels anymore!) and you'll feel that fizzy feeling start already. There is a device called the orgasmatron (no, really) which is designed to do this massaging for you for even more effect, but I prefer to gently use my fingertips.

YOUR OWN RECORDINGS

Here's a thought – why not make your own hypnotic recordings? You could use the script in this manual (great), or invent your own (even better). Then you can add your own suggestions and 'reprogramming' after the induction, then count yourself back to being awake at the end. It's quite easy to do this with programmes like Cool Edit and Audacity if you want to do it on a PC. There's a programme called Vision Guider that is designed for doing exactly this. (See the chapter 'Tools to Help You' for web site links). You could use the record function on an MP3 player, or a good old fashioned tape recorder or voice recorder. If you'd rather have someone else's voice lead you into trance, then you can get hold of the audio programme that accompanies this manual from

www.hypnotic-change.co.uk/FreeYourMind/download.html

and then add your own suggestions on to the end of the induction in there.

MAKING IT EASY

Let's take a look at some ways that we can create even **stronger hypnotic effects.** These are even more cunning ways of bypassing the conscious mind's critical faculty.

One way to increase the hypnotic effect is to use subliminal messages. Now these sound a little scary, perhaps reflecting all the rumours of messages hidden in Beatles records. Like most things, though, it depends how you're going to use this. Way back in the 1950s, scientists did experiments to show how subliminal messages could influence people to behave differently. While the frequently cited example of an experiment where 'Drink Coke' was flashed onto a movie screen, apparently leading to increased sales of the product in the interval, was revealed to have been faked, it does seem that when subliminal messages are used to reinforce something you already wish to do, then it has an effect of strengthening that resolve. It seems clear that at some level subliminal messages work – or at least our advertisers are convinced it does.

Subliminal soundtracks play suggestions at just below the normal level of hearing, so that the unconscious mind is aware of them but the conscious mind can't make enough sense of them to filter them out. I use this a lot on my own hypnosis recordings.

It's also possible to encode 'click tracks' within music so that one ear hears one frequency and one ear hears another slightly different frequency. The mind then does the subtraction between the two to produce the desire brainwave frequency. These are known as binaural beats[4], When combined with some other effects these can be incredibly hypnotic.

---

[4] Binaural beats are so named from 'bi' – two, 'aural' – sound, and 'beats' because the phenomenon of two sounds creating a lower frequency sound is called a 'beat frequency'

We've done several of these, combining subliminal tracks, binaural beats and some very hypnotic sound effects with some fabulous music, and there are some great subliminal tracks available at www.hypnotic-change.com to help you with confidence, insomnia, etc. You can read more in the chapter 'Continuing the Adventure'. We're adding to these tracks all the time, and if there's a particular issue you'd like to tackle, then let us know and we'll look into recording one for you. In fact, we can also provide custom hypnotic tracks for you to deal with the issues you have using some of the imagery you love.

Chapter 15

OTHER ROUTES TO TRANCE

'There is surely nothing other than the single purpose of the moment. A man's whole life is a succession of moment after moment. If one fully understands the present moment, there is nothing left to do, and nothing else to pursue'

- Ghost Dog in 'Ghost Dog'

To be honest, self hypnosis is the easy way. Spiritual seekers have been making use of trance states for thousands of years through meditation practice, and the effects can be spectacular.

One common way of meditating is to concentrate on your breathing, focussing only on the breathing and excluding anything else. If your attention wanders, then that's fine, just let your attention drift back to the rhythm of your breathing and put all your attention there. As you continue to focus only on your breathing, then your mind clears, your breathing slows, and you move into a meditative state very similar to a hypnotic trance.

This is, of course, designed to occupy your conscious mind so that the unconscious can get on with what it wants to do without the conscious poking its nose in where it isn't wanted. Since the superconscious and the unconscious are linked, then this allows a clear channel to Divine energy without the conscious mind being involved at all.

Meditation can therefore bring an incredible level of peace and calm, and will simply let you connect to yourself and the Universe around you in a whole new way.

Of course, there are other ways to occupy the conscious mind. Many meditation schools make use of a mantra for this. A single sound without any conscious meaning is given and repeated (the Buddhist chanting of 'Omm' is an example of a mantra). Again, the conscious mind is occupied with the mantra, leaving the unconscious in peace. Some spiritual groups will provide you with your own personalised mantra which has a meaning known only to the teacher or leader. As I've said before, choose whatever works for you and supports your belief systems. Heavily auditory people will probably find that a mantra will help them – you can either use your own, or get a recording of a mantra from a New Age bookshop.

A different way of doing this which works really well for visual people is to use a mandala. A mandala is a geometric pattern which occupies the visual cortex, allowing (again) the unconscious mind the freedom to play.

Another version of a mandala is to use a lighted candle flame for meditation – the flickering light occupies the mind as the unconscious does its own thing again. Many people will know what it's like to stare into the embers of a fire, or to gather round a campfire or bonfire to watch the flames rise. I personally love this one.

Some people in the meditation community will see the more traditional routes to a meditative state as being more 'spiritual'. I have no idea what that actually means. Whatever we do we are using a process to get into a meditative/trance state. If using self hypnosis makes it easier to get there, then that's all to the good. To my mind the real distinguishing factor is your purpose in all this, and what are you looking to achieve.

Chapter 16

GETTING RESULTS

"You should set a goal big enough that in the process of achieving it, you become someone worth becoming."

- Jim Rohn, US motivational speaker

So. We've learnt how to hypnotise ourselves, you and I, and I have to say that writing these inductions actually had me in a state of trance too. Now, I guess the big question is "so what?" What can we actually DO with self hypnosis? What results can we actually achieve? So let's explore that for a while

RELAXATION

One of the great uses, and perhaps the simplest, for self hypnosis is to relax you. You can use this to just catch your breath in a particularly stressful day, for example. Or you could use it to centre yourself before you go into a challenging meeting or presentation. You could use it to get yourself ready for a sales call.

I quite often use self hypnosis as a quick energizer half way through the day. Many high achievers, including people like Thomas Edison, Albert Einstein and John D Rockefeller used to take power naps throughout the day, and this is my version. In my experience, this works even better – and faster – than a power nap, which can leave you feeling groggy.

It's also often the case that we are mentally exhausted rather than physically exhausted – all we need to do is to allow the mind to 'turn off' for a moment and you'll be naturally refreshed and relaxed really quickly. I used to do this while commuting on the train, even when standing up – I would just relax myself to the point at which I 'nodded off' – at which point I would wake up, because I was standing up – and suddenly I was awake and refreshed again.

To powernap using self hypnosis, simply use the tense and relax method and then count yourself down from (say) 36 to 1 using the yardstick. Have the intention that when you reach the end of the yardstick you will be refreshed and fully alert. This acts as a sure fire rapid refresher that you can fit in with a trip to the bathroom, or a coffee break – no-one even knows you're gone!

You can, of course, also use self hypnosis to help you sleep. As I've said before, this works really well in airplanes, buses, trains – anywhere you might want to nod off and catch up on a few 'Z's. Just relax deeply with the intention of just drifting off to sleep. If you feel your eyes are tired then just cup your hands over your eyes for a few moments before you start.

Regular self hypnosis sessions can beat stress, leaving you in control of your emotions and allowing you space to relax. Often, when we try and consciously relax, our stress response gets even stronger – with self hypnosis the conscious mind is detached from the process, and it gets easier to relax and let go.

Students of mediation suggest that 20 minutes of mediation is equivalent to around 2 hours sleep, so this is a great way to get some well earned extra hours kip.

SEEKING ANSWERS

Wouldn't it be great if we had a way of getting answers to some of the problems that face us? Wouldn't it be terrific to have more options available to us to solve some of the challenges that we have? Self-hypnosis really does give us the chance to connect with a greater consciousness in solving problems.

Dr Elmer R Gates was an incredible inventor in the late 1800s. He invented the foam fire extinguisher and made major improvements to the electric iron and air conditioning. Dr Gates used to go and sit in a room that was soundproofed and dark and literally 'sit for ideas'. With all normal sensory input removed, the ideas and inventions came thick and fast. So much so, in fact, that many American organisations would employ him to do just that. What Dr Gates was doing was finding a way to connect himself to his unconscious mind, and once he had, the ideas would appear almost by magic.

We can achieve the same thing through self hypnosis.

Here's why it works.

Our unconscious mind has access to much, much more data than our conscious mind. Remember that our unconscious stores all our memories – so it has access to a huge library of information and experience that our conscious mind often cannot reach. What's more, many researchers suggest that the unconscious mind stores EVERY piece of information and experience that we ever have. (Now if that sounds incredible, just consider that we are only a few years off having a hand held computer that will store every single piece of media ever created. Every film, every TV programme, every radio broadcast – the lot. Not so unlikely now, is it?!)

What's more, our unconscious tends to think laterally – that is, many things at once. It can see solutions that otherwise we just would not see, because of our conscious mind's linear approach. It gets even better. Our unconscious mind is the home of our imagination, our intuition, of hunches, of leaps in the dark. Setting that creativity free allows us huge leaps of inductive reasoning that we wouldn't make consciously.

Here's more. The unconscious tends to think without the boundaries. Have you ever done that puzzle where you have to join 9 dots with only 4 straight lines - without taking your pen off the paper. It's impossible… until you think outside the confines of the puzzle itself – until you think outside of the box. It's the unconscious mind that makes these leaps, ignoring the rules, playing without limits.

The puzzle:

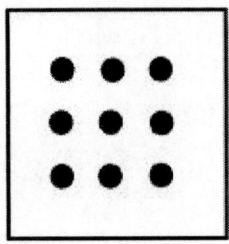

Join each dot with no more than four straight lines, without letting your pen off the paper

The solution:

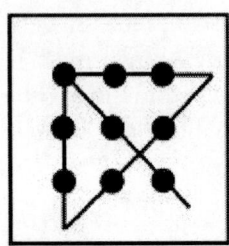

Incidentally… can you do it with three lines?

The unconscious also works in terms of pictures and symbols, stories and images – which means that this opens up a whole new way of creatively solving problems, by using thought processes that the conscious, bound by logic and reason, cannot find.

And finally, if you choose to believe it, the unconscious mind connects you beyond yourself. It enables you to connect to the vast sea of past present and future knowledge to create answers where there were none before. It connects us to Divine power and knowledge, opening up answers that we would never have logically stumbled upon.

So, if you are looking for a solution to a problem of a challenge that faces you – just go into a hypnotic trance and ask your unconscious to reveal the answer. Put a time frame on the question and then just let it go. Sure enough, a solution is going to pop up for you that will answer the question perfectly – you may find that solution comes in a couple of days or a couple of hours, or even sooner than that.. but it'll come.

IMPROVING PERFORMANCE

You can use self hypnosis to make massive differences to your performance in all sorts of areas. Want to improve your golf game? No problem. Looking to get a better tennis shot? Simple. Looking to improve your karate or ju-jitsu? Piece of cake.

Way back, scientists at the University of Chicago experimented with teams of basketball players. One group played basketball as usual, practicing shooting hoops as they normally would. Another group did no practice at all. A third group did no physical practice, but visualised shooting hoops. When they compared their performance in practice, they found that the third group, who visualised but did no practice, had made as much improvement (24%) as those who practiced an hour every day. Now, what would happen if you practiced AND visualised...?

When we look at exactly what's going on, we find that what happens when you imagine is that the same muscle groups fire, the same neurological connections are made, identically to what happens when you do it for real. Your unconscious cannot distinguish between something that's real and something that's vividly imagined.

Of course, the team that visualised saw themselves getting a successful basket each time. So when they came to play, their muscles just assumed that they would make successful baskets.

They had a frame of reference in which they only saw success – whereas the group that practiced actually had a frame of reference for both success and failure, because some of their shots didn't make it. If you practiced physically and had a frame of reference for repeated success, wouldn't that be powerful?

So how does this work for you? Well, simply put you can improve your performance in sport by visualising your success repeatedly over and over. See yourself making that perfect putt, that drive right down the fairway. See yourself getting that serve straight down the line and serving aces repeatedly.

You can work on parts of your game too – if you're looking to improve your backhand for example, then you can focus on that. See those perfect backhand returns going straight down the line.

Now, you can do this without hypnosis. It's just that when you throw hypnosis in it works even better. Take yourself into a hypnotic trance, and then visualise yourself playing the perfect game. Do it over and over to condition your both your mental muscles and your physical responses.

I used to do exactly this technique to get my karate black belt. As I commuted to work I used to imagine myself going through every single move in the 25 kata (set forms) that we had to learn. As I did this I got faster and better at each technique. Similarly, I would see myself responding in kumite (free sparring) and able to respond to my opponents attacks quickly and effectively.

Which means, that when you visualise, you can actually get improved results without actually practicing. Now if you do both, if you visualise AND practice, you can create massive changes.

Now, here's something to make this even more powerful. When you think of yourself being successful, you have a picture. It doesn't matter what the picture is, but we tend to represent the picture to ourselves with what are called 'submodalities' – the attributes of the picture, if you will. (By the way, this works for feelings and sounds you might hear as well). So a picture might be colour, or black and white. It might be near, or far away. It might be in focus or fuzzy. Now, by intensifying the submodalities you can increase the power of the picture. So try making the picture larger, make the colours brighter and more vivid. Make it crystal clear and pin sharp. Make any sounds you can hear clearer and more melodic. Give them a rhythm. Make the feelings that you feel powerful and strong, deepen the feeling and let it flow through your body. Step into the picture and see it as if you are seeing it through your own eyes.

Now, not everyone responds to submodalities in the same way, so play with the picture, with the sounds, with the feelings, until they feel stronger for you. It's *your* imagination – it's your picture.

IN LIFE

So, you might be asking, "does this work in the rest of life?" The answer is, absolutely, yes. You can use this to improve your performance in business, in your personal life, in your relationships…

For example, if you are going to go into a meeting and make an important sales pitch, visualise it. First of all, relax yourself into a hypnotic trance. Then imagine yourself going in to that meeting. Imagine the people there. Imagine them greeting you, and you sitting down or standing in front of them. Imagine your sales pitch, fluent and confident. Imagine your response to their questions. You have the perfect answer to each of their questions, and you answer with certainty and clarity. Then imagine them signing the order and shaking your hand. Make the visualisation truly juicy and exciting. Make it vibrant. Give it colour and depth.

Now, first of all you are going to find that the meeting goes far better than it would have done – in fact you're going to find that it goes very much along the lines that you visualised. Take notes of the questions that you get in your visualisation, because **those questions are likely to be the ones that come up** in real life. Now, I'm not saying that in some way you're able to read the future, or that you've got a direct connection to the people who are going to be at the meeting. I'm not even suggesting that this helps you understand people's concerns better. Perhaps all I'm saying is that your unconscious mind is given free rein to find some answers. What I *am* saying is that it works. Try it!

Now this works in your personal life too. Imagine yourself approaching that cute guy or girl at the bar. Imagine the conversation going really well.. you're witty, you're charming, you're interesting. Imagine them smiling back at you. Imagine them giving you their phone number. Imagine what you like...

Same might go for conversations with your family, or with friends. You could visualise before you start doing your accounts that you're going to find it really easy and you're going to be able to complete the accounts easily and accurately. I used this while writing this manual. I visualised myself writing it easily and naturally, and I visualised myself answering the sorts of questions that people would ask. That made it much easier to put the manual together.

Here's a great one – what about learning? You can dramatically improve your learning ability simply by going into a hypnotic trance and imagining yourself easily understanding what the class is about. Imagine yourself asking incisive questions that give you even more learnings and help the rest of the class to understand better too. Imagine your mind storing away all the information that you've learnt in a really tidy, easy to access way, so that you can access and make use of that learning easily and effortlessly.

(By the way, the ideal learning state is in Hakalau – you can use Hakalau when you are reading a book, or listening to a lecture, or taking a class. Using your peripheral vision will dramatically improve your learning and integration abilities.)

Try hypnotic visualisation on absolutely anything you want to achieve. Simply go into a hypnotic trance, visualise your success, then write down any learnings you have from the experience. You'll find that your performance naturally improves, and you get some fabulous insights and learning too.

HABITS AND ADDICTIONS

You can absolutely use self hypnosis to help you deal with things like cigarette smoking or weight loss.

For weight loss, for example, you might imagine yourself eating more healthily. You might imagine yourself going to the gym and enjoying healthy exercise. You might imagine how much more energy you'll have as you develop a healthier lifestyle. Note that all of these are focussed on the end state. They don't talk about 'losing weight' (who wants to 'lose' anything?! They just focus on what you want, and where you're going, and allow you to enjoy the experience of being a healthy weight up front... and your body gets to like the feeling, and wants more of it.

Same for smoking. Imagine yourself being in a situation where you would normally have a cigarette, and simply not wanting to. Imagine yourself as a non-smoker again. Imagine fresh air flowing into your lungs, cleaning out the dirt and the soot, restoring the beautiful pinkness of the lungs. Imagine your blood flowing through your arteries and your veins, removing the fur from the cigarette deposits. Imagine the energy you will have as you breathe clearly and easily.

PAIN CONTROL

Surgeons increasingly use hypnosis in place of anaesthetics for operations. If you think about it, it's all about relaxation, isn't it? Using hypnosis the normal responses of the nerves can be isolated, allowing for control of pain. Many mothers prefer a hypnosis approach in childbirth, as there are no drugs to affect their unborn baby.

You can make use of self hypnosis to help with pain control, and here are some thoughts to help you.

First of all, you can simply let the pain go. Tell your body that the reasons for that pain are gone, and that you no longer need the reminder. Thank your body for helping you to recognise the problem. Then just allow the pain to leave, feeling it drain out of you. There's no need to push it away, just let it leave naturally, dissolving away. This works really well for headaches and stress pains, of course, because you've acknowledged to your body that you've been listening to what it's trying to tell you.

If it's not obvious, you might want to ask your unconscious mind what the pain is there for. Now here, it's worthwhile remembering that the unconscious mind is quite literal. So "carrying the weight of the world on his shoulders" might actually translate into a pain in your shoulders. "Not standing up for yourself" might actually translate into a pain in the legs. I had eczema problems with my feet until I learnt to 'step forward' with confidence. Richard Moat, founder of Moativational Medicine, would further suggest that the right hand side relates to male influences, while the left hand side relates to female influences. So maybe a pain in your left hand is a result of a reluctance to reach out to your mother or to your wife.

You might try repeating a mantra such as "totally numb, free of pain" to yourself over and over. This has the effect of jamming the pain signals. This can be incredibly effective. For example, when firewalkers walk on flaming hot coals, they often repeat phrases like "cool moss" to jam the internal dialogue, and cause the mind to think about something other than the fact that they are walking on burning coals.

Another technique that works really well is to think of three words to describe the pain. For example, you might think 'searing', 'stabbing', and 'intense'. Then think of another three words – like 'uncomfortable', 'jabbing', 'sore'. Then another three words, and so on. You'll find that as you go, the words that you use become less intense and less powerful – and so does the pain.

You could perhaps let yourself drift above the pain. Just imagine yourself floating out of your body and observing the pain. Or you might like to imagine the affected part or the pain itself floating away from your body.

Finally, you can use a technique known as 'location elimination'. Rather than trying to get rid of the pain, visualise cutting the location of that pain in half. If you have a headache, imagine that the headache is in the right half of your head.. then perhaps in the front of your head.. then just above your eye, then in the corner of your eye.. just let it get smaller and smaller. It doesn't need to disappear, just let if shrink.. When it's shrunk to be tiny, the pain will disappear too. You can then imagine it leaving your body in some way.

Just one word of caution on pain control. Pain is the body's way of letting you know that something is wrong. Make sure you've consulted your doctor about chronic pain, and use self hypnosis alongside any medical treatment rather than to replace it.

LEARNING

Because it allows you to use your whole mind, hypnosis can be an incredible aid for learning, enabling people to take in information much more readily with better recall and comprehension. You can also enable the unconscious mind to help you in test taking too.

We've already talked about Hakalau as being the learning state, and how it enables you to absorb information more easily. All information and experiences that you have are stored in your unconscious mind for retrieval. Now, stress is one thing that prevents you from recalling what you need. Have you ever had something "on the tip of your tongue" and yet you can't remember it, try as you might? Yet hours later, when you've forgotten about it and you're no longer stressed about it, the information just swims into your awareness. Now, of course, you can use self hypnosis to relax you and recall the information quickly. Since you have a body memory of what relaxation feels like, you can just drop into that feeling, even in the middle of a conversation, and recall the information.

This is the key to test taking, by the way… just relax. Your body will recall things much more easily if you are relaxed and calm – so, again, Hakalau and deep breathing will relax you to take the test.

REMEMBERING

Have you ever had one of those moments where you simply can't think where you put something? No matter how much you charge around the house, you simply can't find your car keys/wallet/glasses/mobile phone?

This was me – in fact, one of my colleagues suggested that she tie my wallet on one end of a piece of string and my mobile phone on the other, and then thread the string down my sleeves – the same way as some kids used to have their gloves on a piece of string. And just ask my boys about how many times I've charged round the house looking for my things.

Well, here's the thing. Your unconscious mind (the bit that's responsible for memory, remember?) know exactly where you put them. It's just that your increasing stress level won't let you access that information.

So, simply by relaxing, going through the self hypnosis drill that you've learnt, you will allow your unconscious mind to bring those memories to your awareness, and you'll know where your keys/wallet/phone have got to… and you'll be surprised to know that they don't sneak off on their own accord while no-one's watching. In fact, you'll probably find that your unconscious (or intuition, if you like) tells you something and you don't believe it – until you actually go and look there. I predict the conversation will go along the lines of 'they can't be there, I haven't even been in that room' or 'they can't be there, I haven't worn that coat for ages'.

This works quite well when something is 'on the tip of your tongue'. You just can't remember the name of that movie star, or that book you read, or the name of a street. I know you've had this experience, haven't you. The more you strive, the less you can remember. But when you relax, suddenly it all comes back. That's why you wake up in the middle of the night and yell 'Highfield Road' or 'Annie Lennox' – because you've relaxed, the unconscious mind has been able to get a word in edge ways.. and bingo!

MORE ON MEMORY

There are many books available that provide memory techniques to help you remember lists of items, names, numbers and so on. All these techniques are great, although sometimes they seem a little cumbersome. Derren Brown's book 'Tricks of the Mind' has some neat tools that you can use to improve your memory. It's worthwhile looking into these.

I'd like to suggest something that will make those techniques even more effective – and may even be enough for your purposes. The secret is to relax. When you need to remember something, just let your body relax using the tools you've learnt. Then commit the list, the phone number, the task, the name, whatever it is to memory. When you need to recall it, then just relax again.

This works two ways. Firstly, relaxation aids memory, allowing the conscious and unconscious to work together, as we've already noted. Secondly, memory is 'state dependent'. When we memorise something, we seem to make our emotional state part of the key to recovering that memory. If we're not in the same emotional state, then it becomes tricky to recall it.

This is why we can walk into the kitchen and forget why we've gone there. We've moved from one emotional state to another, and lost the key. So if you want to remember something, get back into the state you were when you committed it to memory. This is why 'exam panic' causes people to forget – they memorised the information in a relaxed state, and now they are trying to recall it in a tense state. It makes it more difficult to get access to the information.

So, when you're learning, make sure that you're relaxed, and then when you need to recall the information, relax again. Suddenly your memory gets access and you can recall things easily.

AND THERE'S MORE

There are all sorts of applications to self hypnosis – use your imagination(!) and come up with new applications that help you. If you think self hypnosis may be able to help you with something, it probably can (otherwise why would your unconscious have given you that idea in the first place?)

Chapter 17

GET WHERE YOU WANT TO GO

"Live your life as if your dreams had come true, and then challenge

reality to catch up"

- Topher Morrison, US hypnotherapist

SETTING INTENTIONS

We can use self hypnosis to effectively set intentions and goals for ourselves. One thing we want to do when we set a goal is to give ourselves the means to achieve it. There are many, many goal setting techniques, and goal setting programmes such as S-M-A-R-T which is familiar to many from management seminars and NLP training courses, along with 'Keys to Achievable Outcomes'. You can find these in the Further Resources section on Goal Setting. These help you to set effective goals, but don't really assist you with the process of actually achieving that goal. It's a bit like streamlining a car – you can streamline a Porsche to make it as aerodynamic as you like, to make it as easy to move through the air as possible – but without an engine it's not going to go anywhere.

So wouldn't it be useful if we could **activate part of our brain that will increase our chances of success** and act as an autopilot to helping us achieve our goals? Welcome to the reticular activating system or RAS.

Have you ever played that game called 'Bug Blaster' in the car? You simply have to look out for Volkswagen Beetles on the road and shout when you see one. Now, here's the thing – as soon as you start playing the game, suddenly the road is full of Volkswagen Beetles. They didn't suddenly turn up from the great games organiser in the sky – it's just that you've started noticing them more. This is the RAS at work. You've effectively programmed the RAS with an instruction of "find me all the Volkswagen Beetles" and the RAS has dutifully gone about its task. It's a bit like a guided missile locking on to its target – it will automatically find what it's seeking.

Exactly the same thing happens when we're looking for a new job or a new house – we're idly looking through the newspaper and suddenly an advertisement 'leaps out' at us. Again, the RAS is bringing things to your attention that you've told it to look out for.

So wouldn't it be great if we could find a way of easily programming the RAS to help us get our goals. You'll find, as you do, that the RAS will sift through all the information that's coming in and help you notice the useful things when they are spotted by the RAS. It's going to grab on to resources that will help you and bring them to your notice. Cool or what?

So here's what to do – when you've got your goal set properly (see the Further Resources section on goal setting for more information) then go into a hypnotic state and simply tell your unconscious mind what the goal is. You could say something like "I want to move to a four bedroom detached house by the end of the summer of 2008". Then the RAS will lock onto this goal and start searching for opportunities that will match that. It might find suitable houses as you drive around, or as you read the paper, or it might spot opportunities that you hadn't even thought of for house exchange. In the movie 'The Secret', John Assaraf recounts the story of how he set an intention to attract a particular type of house, and he had a picture of the sort of house he wanted to help trigger his RAS. One day he suddenly realised that he'd actually moved into the exact same house that was in the picture. Now that's autopilot!

Now, just a brief word on goal setting affirmations here. I want to dismiss the complicated debate about **how to phrase your affirmations**.

Some people believe that you should set a goal *in the future*, so that your unconscious mind knows to move towards it. So they would say something like "I am finding ways to increase my income by £20,000 per year" or whatever. The goal is clearly stated as being in the future, so that the unconscious mind says "OK, I need to do something here" and moves towards the goal.

Others believe that you should set a goal *as if you have already achieved it*. This, they say, activates the unconscious mind so that it wants to close the reality gap between what you say and what you have, much as an elastic band will want to snap back into place when you stretch it. Many supporters of this approach would also say that when you start to create the feelings of having what you want, then this attracts the thing itself – this is the Law of Attraction, or the Cosmic Ordering Service: decide what you want, ask the Universe to provide it, and then, as you feel the feelings of already having it, the vibrations of energy that you set up attract the goal to you. So you might write a goal as "I am enjoying my new income of £100,000 per year" (for example) on the basis that your unconscious – and the Universe – will try and close the gap. Or they might write "I am so happy and grateful that I have an income of over £100,000 per year". It's beyond the scope of this manual to go into this in detail, although the chapter on 'Continuing Your Journey' has some more reading material for you on the subject of The Law of Attraction.

I have to say that I tend to write my goals as "I thank God for my new detached house with four bedrooms" as this then connects me to Divine power and allows me to live in a world of gratitude and thankfulness. The energy and the feeling of experiencing my goal goes out into the Universe and attracts the reality to match the feeling I already have.

So what should you do? Whatever you feel is best. Think about it – if we have this incredible, powerful creative consciousness, I think **it can work out what we mean when we set a goal**. So the keys for me are:

- ☐ Do you really want it?

- ☐ Do you know exactly what you want?

- ☐ Can you describe it fully?

- ☐ Do you know when you want it?

- ☐ Is that goal good for you, for others, and for the planet?

- ☐ Am I grateful for having it?

And then I get on and use that goal as an intention.

So, let's say I want to increase my income by £20,000 per year. I'll want to give my mind plenty to work on, so I will want to set it a task of

- ☐ Discover what options there are to increase my income

- ☐ What ideas could I have to increase my income?

- ☐ What am I already doing to create that income?

- ☐ What else could I be doing to create that income?

- ☐ What contacts can I make to create that income?

And so on

Then I go into self hypnosis and simply relax – while in the trance, I give my unconscious mind the instructions to reach the goal… and then I just **let go of all attachment to that goal**. I might say something to myself like "and now I simply let go of all attachment to this goal, and I allow my unconscious mind to find ways for it to come to pass"

CREATE EXCITING GOALS

If you are working on suggestions to help you when you're pursuing your goals, then make sure they are truly compelling and exciting for you.

If your goal is to make more money, then what will that money enable you to do? Money by itself isn't exciting for most of us – but what it will help us buy IS! Think about what you will be able to do, the adventures you can have, the things it will enable you to achieve.

Some of you will probably be asking the question "what if I get the details wrong? What if the perfect car/house/holiday/cash windfall is out there and I didn't get the details absolutely right?" Well, make sure you're asking for **"that or something even better"** and let go of attachment to the outcome. Here's the thing. Your mind knows what you're really looking for, and it will go out there and find the things that match what you really want.

- ☐ Who is going to be with you?

- ☐ What colour car would you like?

- ☐ When do you want the money by?

- ☐ Where would you like to go on holiday?

- ☐ What sort of house do you want?

And so on.

LETTING GO

OK, now here's something to weave in to your goal setting process – and I did mention it a bit earlier. Here's something that will make a massive difference to the effects you get when you go for your goal. And it's really simple.

Let it go.

Really.

Let it go.

It might seem odd that once you've set a goal that you should just let it go, yet this is an incredibly powerful part of the process. Here's why.

When we are holding on to a goal, we are actually connecting ourselves to the energy and the emotion of not having it. Every time we think about that goal, we say 'I want that', or 'why hasn't that happened yet'. We worry about what we need to do to achieve it. We actually experience the lack of it. It's a bit like delegating a task and then checking every ten minutes to see how it's going. The unconscious mind simply says 'well if you know how to do it, just get on with it yourself then'.

When we let go of it, then our unconscious mind is freed up to make the connections and take the actions necessary to bring it to us. The unconscious draws in the resources that we need. It has free rein to go where it needs and draw in what it needs.

CHANGE YOUR LIFE

"When your desires are strong enough you will appear to possess superhuman powers to achieve."

- Napoleon Hill, US author

Many people look to hypnosis to make changes in their life that they've failed to do using the power of their conscious minds and their willpower. I don't know what that might be for you.

It might be that you want to give up smoking. Now, as I'm sure you know, hypnosis has been used to help people give up smoking for a long time and with great success. You need to know that hypnosis can only support you in doing something that you want to do. So if you've been badgered into giving up, then it's not going to be very effective, because your conscious desires are battling the reprogramming. If, however, you really do want to give up, then hypnosis can support you. You may just need to look at the positive benefits for you of giving up. What will you do with all that money? How much fresher will your breath (and your clothes) be? How much healthier will you be?

It might be that you want to lose weight, or eat more healthily. Again, if you really have a great goal of being healthy, and it isn't just that you feel guilty, then hypnosis will really help you. If you *are* doing this through guilt, then you simply need to think how your life will be better when you're a healthy weight. How much better will you feel? Will you have more energy and feel more alive? Will you be able to get into that fabulous dress? Will you feel good on the beach? Build up the positives

You can use hypnosis to deal with compulsions, for example.

You might be looking for hypnosis to help with pain control. Now one thing I will say straight off the bat is that hypnosis can really help with pain control: for example headaches, period pain, migraines can all respond really well to self hypnosis. However, if you're looking at chronic pain, then make sure your doctor is involved and fully informed, and use self hypnosis to support what the medics are doing.

Or perhaps you're really lacking in confidence. You might really struggle in one to one situations, or when faced with larger meetings. You might 'freeze' in social situations, or when you meet someone new.

So, how do you work with these kinds of issues?

Well, first of all, you need to make sure you have some really compelling end result imagery. What do you want instead? How will it feel when you have the result you want? More importantly, what will you be DOING. Here's something important – you can't simply erase the old behaviour, whether it's smoking, or eating unhealthily, or feeling nervous around people. You've got to have a new behaviour to program. So how will it be when you've got what you want? How much better will YOUR life be? Not your spouse's life, or your children's life, or your boss's life – YOUR life.

Really spend some time on this one. Make it as juicy, compelling and exciting as you possibly can. We're going to look a bit more at how to create compelling imagery in a moment, but for now, really get an idea of what you want instead of your current behaviour.

Then it's quite simple. You just go into a hypnotic state, and focus on the behaviour you're going to do instead. Consider how easy it's going to be to achieve what you want. Imagine yourself doing exactly what you plan, easily and with loads of enjoyment.

Then think about how it's going to feel when you've got what you want. Really feel the feelings that you're going to feel then. Imagine what you're going to see, and hear the sounds you're going to hear when you're behaving the way you want. Cool, isn't it?

So, for example if you want to lose weight, you might imagine how easy it's going to be to eat healthy food; how simple it's going to be to stop eating when you're feeling satisfied; how much you're going to enjoy all the tastes that you're going to experience. Then you'd consider how it will be when you've achieved your goal and you're at your perfect weight. What will you be doing, who will you be talking to? Will you be out dancing or getting exercise?

POWERFUL SUGGESTIONS

OK, you want to get hold of the most powerful suggestions possible to help you get the results you want. So how can you produce suggestions that really work?

Make it constructive

Well, first of all, make sure that they are positive suggestions. Here's why. Firstly, the unconscious mind can't accept a negative – so it's going to focus on what you don't want (I don't want to smoke, I don't want to be overweight, I don't want low self esteem etc) – and what you focus on is what you get. So you're going to end up fatter, smoking more and being more nervous!

Look for the things you want not the things you don't want. You want to say

"I'll be healthier" not "I won't be overweight"

"I'll be full of confidence" not "I won't be nervous"

"I'll have lots of energy" not "I won't feel so tired"

Give your mind something really positive to go for, and it will.

Let's see action

Now, instead of describing feelings, what are you going to be DOING? Describe what your future will be like in action terms.

So if you're going to be healthier, what will that enable you to DO? Will you play more sport? Go walking? Play with the kids more?

If you're going to lose weight, what will that help you do? Shop for dresses that look fabulous? Meet that perfect guy? Show off your perfect pecs on the beach?

If you're going to be more confident, what will that support you doing? Will you be able to get that dream job? Will you be able to go to and enjoy parties? Will you ask that cute girl out?

Whatever it is, look for the action. This will help your body get excited about what it's going to be doing, which means it's going to be supporting you.

Please be specific

Finally, you want to be specific. What specifically will you be doing? For example, who will be with you? Where will you be? This will help you create really compelling scenes of how things will be in the future

Until you've got something specific to work towards, your unconscious mind doesn't know what you're looking for.

Being specific allows your mind more details to pursue and makes the images more exciting and inspiring.

So if you're imagining yourself out in your new, healthy, svelte body playing volleyball on the beach:

- ☐ Who are you playing with?

- ☐ What are you wearing?

- ☐ Where is the beach?

- ☐ How do you feel?

And so on.

If you're imagining yourself giving a great presentation because you're so confident:

- ☐ Who's in the audience?

- ☐ What are you speaking about?

- ☐ What's the hall like?

- ☐ Do they love your presentation? (of course they do!)

And so on.

Add in details, even if they don't seem to be particularly relevant. It doesn't matter. The unconscious mind will build on the picture – the more vivid it is, the more interesting it's going to be, and the more that you'll engage the unconscious mind. What colours are there? What details are there? What are the sounds? What are the feelings you have?

So, when you are looking to change a behaviour, whether it's comfort eating, nail biting, smoking, feeling nervous – whatever it is – then you want to look at two things:

- ☐ What will you need to do differently?

- ☐ What will you do instead?

Make the images of what you are going to do instead - truly exciting, inspiring and thrilling for you. Make them positive, make sure they have action, and make them specific. That way you're going to create something for your unconscious to lock onto and turn into reality.

METAPHORS AND STORIES

As we're growing up, we loved stories, didn't we? Even now we're older, we still love the mesmerising power of a well woven story – transporting us to a new and exciting world. Again, the story bypasses our consciousness and lets our unconscious get to grips with incredibly juicy imagination. In stories, anything is possible, isn't it? In stories you can be who you want to be, do what you want. Normal rules no longer apply.

So when you're working with the unconscious, you can use metaphor and stories. Instead of telling the unconscious mind directly what to do, you can use a metaphor instead. So, let's say you want to deal with a fear of public speaking through self hypnosis. You might decide that what you want instead of fear is *confidence, wisdom* and *calm*.

You might construct a story about a kind yet shy noble prince who, instead of claiming his inheritance as king and heir to the throne, decided to run away to a far off land and live there, unrecognised and in secret. He passed his days working hard on the land – although it was an honest job, it was hard work, and sometimes he felt that he missed the life of privilege and power that he had been used to. Always, though, when he thought of going home, he realised that he would have to take his place as king, and would be expected to rule and lead his people. One day, however, he saw a great crowd of people trudging away from the city. They had been sent away because no-one would speak up for them. Seeing their distress, the prince decided that someone must speak for them, and a great sense of peace came over him as he wove a vision of the life that could be theirs if they turned round and demanded their rights. Swayed by his confidence and by his persuasive words, the crowd turned back and, with the prince at their head, set off for the city. When they arrived, the prince spoke on their behalf, and his words demonstrated so much insight and power that the city rulers readily agreed to his terms. Word of his exploits eventually made its way back to his own city, where an emissary was sent to ask if he would return – where he ruled with great wisdom for many years.

So the essence of metaphor is to take the situation that you are faced with, and decide what outcome you would want from that situation. Now take that goal, and weave a story around it. Take it into the past, or take it into the future. You can invoke ancient myths, or you can use up to date language and street scenes.

The point is that you are engaging YOUR imagination. It's YOUR story, and you can tell it how YOU want. There are no rules: the goal is to make sure that at the end of the story you experience the emotional state that you want to have in reality.

One of my teachers told a wonderful story for smoking cessation about a castle, grey and stained, overgrown and unloved. His metaphor explained how the occupants opened up the castle gates and cleared out the garbage inside. As they cleared and cleaned, they revealed beautiful translucent marble, veined in rich colours, shining and bright. They opened up all the doors and let the castle breathe again, and let the air sweep the castle clean of years of neglect.

And so on. The only limit is YOUR imagination – so reconnect with your inner kid and tell yourself a story.

Chapter 18

BEYOND OURSELVES

"Intent is a force that exists in the universe. When sorcerers (those who live of the Source) beckon intent, it comes to them and sets up the path for attainment, which means that sorcerers always accomplish what they set out to do."

-*Carlos Castaneda, South American shaman*

CONNECT TO A HIGHER POWER

I was a little bit hesitant to include this section in a manual on self hypnosis and that's for two reasons.

Firstly, of course, self hypnosis works chance whether you believe in a higher power or not. The concepts of conscious and unconscious mind have been so well documented over the years, and hypnosis is so startlingly effective, that there's no need to believe in God, or the Divine, or the Universal power in order to make it work.

Secondly, for those of us who do believe in God, the whole question of using self hypnosis to help us in our pursuit of spirituality can seem a little 'mechanical' or 'unspiritual'. Well, for me walking is a pretty normal and mechanical pursuit, but it's yielded me some of the most incredible spiritual insights that I have ever had.

Having said that, I make no apologies for including this. Atheists can ignore it (skip to the next chapter, folks), agnostics can make up their own mind about it (unless they don't) and spiritual seekers can incorporate the pieces that work for them. As with everything in this magical world of self hypnosis – it's up to you!

So, how does self hypnosis link with spirituality? Well, I believe that the superconscious mind is continually directly linked to God, or Divine Intelligence. It's simply the way we were created, to be made in the image of God, and that means that we're directly linked to the Creator. What's more, the unconscious is pretty cool with that too – it's happy to go along with whatever the superconscious or the conscious tells it. Only problem is, the conscious mind is busy taking control, being logical, looking for scientific answers, being rational. So the conscious mind is actually acting as a barrier between ourselves and the spiritual world.

So, if we can just get the conscious mind out of the way for a while, then we have a chance of letting God in and for us contacting a Higher Power. The conscious mind is going to be forever saying "that doesn't make sense" and "don't be silly" – so let's give the rest of our minds chance to breathe and experience everything that can be experienced.

This is what the ancients have always been doing with meditation. It's simply a way of getting the conscious mind out of the way and helping us connect with a spiritual dimension. Same with self hypnosis – it's the same thing, just approached from a different direction. The only real difference between self hypnosis and meditation seems to be that self hypnosis has a goal and tends to be active, whereas meditation tends not to have a specific goal and tends to be passive. Apart from the times where that's not true.

So let's assume for the moment that self hypnosis and meditation lead to the same place – a greater connection with the spiritual world, with God – you use the words that work best for you.

So what can we do with this? Well, let's see….

RECEIVING INSPIRATION

Well, one thing is that we're opening a channel to communicate at a deeper spiritual level. By connecting ourselves up to a Higher Power, then it's not just going to be our own minds that are working on this. We can get input from Higher Intelligence — and we can get input from the rest of humanity, past and present. So if you're looking for an answer to something, you can trust that the answer is going to come, and not just from inside your unconscious. There will be times when you feel truly inspired, when something leaps into your consciousness that you would never have considered otherwise. And you will be truly connected to something that's greater than yourself.

So when you're looking for a solution, drop into self hypnosis and ask the question. The answer will turn up: you can choose to attribute this to your unconscious mind, to God, to the Universe, or to coincidence. All you need to do is to trust what you've been given — and act on it.

REMOTE VIEWING

For many years man has been looking for a way to reach across time and space. Whether that's through telepathy or through Star Trek teleportation, man has been looking for a way to extend his reach — to go beyond where he is and what he can experience.

In the 1960s and 70s, both America and Russia carried out many experiments on remote viewing, remote influence and telepathy. Many of those were incredibly successful. For example, a volunteer would be despatched to a randomly chosen remote location. The viewer would then connect - at a psychic level - to the volunteer and describe what the volunteer could see. The results were often spookily accurate. On Apollo 14, Ed Mitchell carried out experiments to see if he could transmit images (of the classic Zener symbols (square, circle, star, cross, wavy lines) used in telepathy experiments) back to earth using his mind — again, with statistically very significant results.

So, try this, and enjoy the experience.

First of all, think of a place that you want to view remotely. It might be an office you are going to visit, or a holiday destination. It might even be somewhere like the road home to see if there are traffic jams. You might want to connect with a loved one half way round the world.

Go into self hypnosis and then imagine a fog or a mist in front of you. That fog or mist is all that separates you from being where you want to be, and seeing what you want to see. Decide to pierce that mist – watch as the mist swirls and spins, and a tunnel opens up. It might be lit with blue or white light, and you might be able to see that light reach through the tunnel. Through the tunnel you can see the location you are thinking of. Describe it to yourself, getting the details: the colours, the location of objects, the people. Hear what's going on and what's being said. You might even be able to sense the smells and tastes of what's going on at the other end. Ask your unconscious if there is anything else that you need to do based on the knowledge that you have gained. When you've finished, let the mists swirl back into place.

As you do this, you'll find that you get better and better at describing the other end of the connection. What's more, you'll find that you gain useful insights from the experience – a decision to take a different route home, or to remember to pack something else for the holiday. You might feel led to pray for someone, or to send healing energy through the tunnel (I'm not going to discuss it here, but many people actively perform remote healing through this sort of connection).

Remember to preserve the learnings from these exercises, and add them to your toolbox.

SUMMING UP

There are a whole series of potential applications for self hypnosis. Let that simply be a starting point, a leaping off point for your exploration of the power of the unconscious mind. You can use self hypnosis in any situation where you need to relax, where you need to eliminate stress. You can use it in any situation where you need to improve your performance, whether that's in business, in sport, or in your personal life. You can use it to leverage the power of your mind, the incredible resources of your conscious, unconscious and superconscious minds. You can use it to connect to the spiritual world and as a meditation. You are only limited by your imagination.

Chapter 19

TOOLS TO HELP YOU

"One only needs two tools in life: WD-40 to make things go, and duct tape to make them stop."

- G. Weilacher

Now, having said that, you might want to get some additional tools to help you with your adventures in Self Hypnosis. Here are some thoughts for you.

Firstly, get hold of an MP3 player (or an ipod if you really must buy one from Apple!). These little devices store loads of music and allow you to replay it anywhere you are. This means you can store thousands of music tracks and use them without taking a stack of CDs with you everywhere. On mine I have lots of relaxing music for hypnosis, including Topher Morrison's WindTrance and NativeTrance which I love, some music by Fridrik Karlsson and others. I have some relaxation tracks that I've created using pzizz (see more in a couple of lines!) and some subliminal recording tracks that I've recorded myself. I've also got quite a lot of training stuff on there too, and some hypnotic inductions and programmes from myself and other hypnotherapists. The end result is that all my audio stuff goes with me. The latest players also include video, which means that I could include video clips which some of us are now putting out to help visual people go into trance. Couple that with a good pair of headphones and you have a really great way to help you go into trance anywhere you like.

One really neat gadget that I've got is pzizz. pzizz is a little hand held device like an MP3 player. It has a software program on it that creates millions of combinations of hypnotic tracks to help you take a 10 minute or 20 minute time out from your day and come back energized. There's also a version to help you drift off to sleep. See www.pzizz.com.

If you don't want to buy the hardware, then you can get a version for your computer. It does exactly the same thing, but allows you to create tracks to download to a regular MP3 player. Highly recommended for that 'pick you up' in the middle of the day, and for power napping.

If you're interested in making your own hypnotic recordings with your own suggestions, then you'll need a good recording program. I use a program called CoolEdit Pro from Adobe – there are some older versions available free. Alternatively, Audacity is a great product and available entirely free. See www.audacity.sourceforge.net. You can use this to mix music and your own suggestions together. You can even create subliminal messages and include those in your own tracks, mixed just below audible level to bypass your conscious mind. There's a great piece of software called Vision Guider (see www.gotvision.com) which is specifically designed to make the process of creating subliminal tracks easier.

I have a range of hypnotherapy tracks available for download, including 'Stop Smoking', 'Absolute Confidence' and 'Peaceful Sleep'. These incredibly powerful hypnotic CDs include some beautiful music and truly powerful suggestions to help you get the results you want. Check out www.hypnotic-change.com for more information on the current range.

If you're interested in a custom hypnosis CD created especially for you with an induction and suggestions created especially for you, and a really cool subliminal track, then drop me an email at tim@theinspirationcentre.com and I'll let you know how to go about ordering a copy.

Chapter 20

THE ADVENTURE CONTINUES

"With great power comes great responsibility"

- Uncle Ben in 'Spiderman'

We all know how the story of Arthur and Merlin ends, don't we? How Arthur learnt from his wise and powerful mentor, how he practiced until the wisdom, and the magic, and the power became part of Arthur's life too. Until it seemed that anything was possible. We hear of Arthur defeating the enemies that faced him, how he brought peace and order to a whole kingdom.

I imagine, in my mind's eye, Merlin watching his student with approval. "You have learnt well, my friend", he said "and you know that you can do these things. Use your new powers wisely – but do use them, use them to create massive changes in your kingdom. Use them to bring peace to others. Use them to serve others. Draw around you men and women who share your vision. Build something new – something that is a true reflection of Who You Are".

And across the mists of time, I can feel Merlin and Arthur watching us all, to see where we recognise magic, and power, and truth. To see if we will follow our dreams.

You know, I always wished I become a superhero like my comic book role models. I wished that I could have special powers. I would love to have saved the world, battling all that's wrong every day, rescuing those in distress. It's funny how that's turned out, really, and though I'm now as bald as Mr X was, I have found a way to live my dreams, and sometimes my life hardly seems real. It's almost as if I'd drawn it myself.

You know, dreams can come true, and the things we want most seem to appear...

And so the teacher roused me from my reverie. "I trust you enjoyed your daydream", he said as I got up to find my next lesson. I was ready for anything, although I paused for a moment to do up the top button on my shirt so that no one could see the costume that was hidden underneath...

Chapter 21

TO THE FUTURE!

"The more you can dream the more you can do."

- Michael Korda, UK/US Playwright

Well, that completes our journey into self hypnosis. It's almost like a brief exploratory trip, where you get ready for the adventure of a life time. There is so much to explore, and so many possibilities. Be curious. Feel free to experiment and try things out. Read books. Find new applications for self hypnosis. Maybe attend a class and learn more. Try out some of the hypnosis products available. There is so much to discover, and so many possibilities for continuing the adventure. We've made a start – it's up to you to carry on the journey. Above all… have fun.

Tim Hodgson

January 2008

Chapter 22

CONTINUING THE ADVENTURE

You are here for no other purpose than to realize your inner divinity and manifest your innate enlightenment.

Morihei Ueshiba, the founder of Aikido

With everything that I have learnt over the years, there's only one thing that I am certain of – that there is always more to learn.

I'd like to give you some great resources for further study, and I hope you'll get some of the books and join me on an incredible journey even further down the rabbit hole....

BOOKS

Settle for Excellence – Topher Morrison. I really love this book by the guy who trained me in hypnotherapy. There are some great insights into how to make changing your life really easy. Not strictly a book on hypnosis, but a lot of what Topher talks about will help you to get what you really want out of life.

Zero Limits – Joe Vitale and Iheakala Hew Len. This book introduced me to Ho'oponopono, the ancient Hawaiian process for creating your perfect life by cleaning your way back to 'zero state' where anything is possible. Some of it is very spooky – but open your mind and hear this incredible message.

The Attractor Factor – Joe Vitale. This book outlines the process of attraction or cosmic ordering. Keep an open mind about how to attract the life you want, and unleash the power of your unconscious to get you there.

The Field – Lynne McTaggart. An incredible book that links the science of quantum physics and zero point energy with spirituality and the supernormal – demonstrating that we are all interconnected.

The Dark Side of the Light Chasers – Debbie Ford. This book will help you understand that even the 'dark side' inside us has to be welcomed with open arms if we are to be whole and attain our true power.

Think and Grow Rich – Napoleon Hill. This little gem from 1937 contains some incredible forward thinking on suggestion, on borrowed genius, and the science of attracting true wealth.

Infinite Mind – Valerie Hunt. A well reasoned book that takes us to the edge of scientific research into the workings of the mind.

The Holographic Universe – Michael Talbot. This book explores the work of Bohm and Pribram, who demonstrated that the world is not really as real as we might think, but also how a holographic model of the universe can explain many psychic phenomena.

Tricks of the Mind - Derren Brown. I don't agree with Derren on many things, but he is the consummate showman, demonstrating the power of the mind in ways that noone has before. Some great stuff on hypnosis, on learning, and on memory.

Paul McKenna – Paul has written many books, including 'Change Your Life in Seven Days', 'I can make you rich', 'I can make you thin' and so on. He uses some great hypnotic principles throughout.

The *Conversations With God* series from Neale Donald Walsch have been instrumental in helping me understand what I believe about the nature of the Universe. Read 'Conversations with God' or 'What God Wants' – but be prepared to have your world view challenged!

MOVIES

There are loads more great movies out there, but some of those I would suggest you watch include:

"What the Bleep Do We Know" – an amazing movie that takes you to places that you've never expected to go – explains quantum physics, the power of emotions, and how to create your reality. There's some great information on how your mind works and the funniest version of "Addicted to Love" that you will ever see. "What the Bleep Do We Know - Down the Rabbit Hole" is an extended edition.

"The Secret" – watch this movie. Available from www.thesecret.tv, this film will give you incredible insights into how to create the life you want using the power of attraction. I've alluded to many of the concepts here, but for more, get the movie or check out the book "The Secret" which contains even more material than the film. The film has its detractors, and I certainly feel it has its limitations, but for an introduction to creating the life you want, it's well filmed with some great contributors.

"The Moses Code" – one step on from "The Secret" and to be honest far more aimed at serving the world rather than serving yourself. It looks at the gift that God gave to Moses that enabled him to liberate the Israelite people from slavery in Egypt.

I'd also recommend you go out and watch films like "Pay It Forward", "It's a Wonderful Life", "Serendipity", "The Matrix" and "A Knight's Tale" – there are some great messages there on how you can change your life.. or someone else's.. or the world. Most movies have some form of morality tale, and I often take some notes on great quotes. Stay open and listen. www.imdb.com is a great source of movie quotes.

Also check out Derren Brown's shows available on DVD. Remember that Derren himself says that his show is a blend of magic, mentalism and illusion, so don't ascribe everything you see to psychic powers!

Youtube.com is a great source of videos on hypnotism, ranging from the convincing to the crazy, the sane to the surreal. Watch with caution. Jamie Smart puts some good stuff up on youtube, and there are often deconstructions of hypnotists like Derren Brown too.

MUSIC

Check out WindTrance and NativeTrance available from www.tophermorrison.com which are great hypnosis tracks. They use the rhythms of lullabies to create hypnotic states.

Fridrik Karlsson has a tremendous range of music for relaxation. Have a look at www.newworldmusic.com to buy and also for other meditation products.

You could also take a look at music from Chris Handley at www.cafepress.com/needtorelax - Chris has some great atmospheric tracks available.

AND FINALLY

Above all, enjoy the adventure. Use what works. Put what doesn't work on one side. Experiment. Play. Learn. Discover. Have fun. This is an incredible journey you are on, and it's one where your success is certain.

Stay in touch. Mail me your success stories. Ask questions. Above all, trust that YOU are incredibly powerful, an amazing being capable of incredible achievements, amazing feats and wonderful wisdom. All you have to do is to let it happen.

Chapter 23

FURTHER RESOURCES

FULL HYPNOSIS SCRIPT

This script is the same as the one in the main text above. I've removed the commentary and occasional witty comment so that you can just read through it. Alternatively, this script is available through www.hypnotic-change.co.uk/FreeYourMind/download.html

for you to use as a guided visualisation into hypnosis..

[INITIAL INDUCTION]

So, find a nice peaceful spot and make yourself comfortable. Let all the distractions just recede into the background, just let them go, you don't need to even have them in your consciousness right now. Just let them disappear from your mind... if you need them later you can pick them up if they are still important, but for right now, just let them go...

Any sounds that you hear are just indicators that you are going even deeper into trance, and becoming even more relaxed.

And if any thoughts should come up, you can feel free to just let those thoughts go too... it's OK, just let them drift off into the distance, you can pick them up later if you need to but for now just let them drift away like clouds in the sky.

Now breathe deeply, a nice deep relaxing breath. Take your time over this wonderful, easy, simple breath. Breathe in for a count of five... then breathe out for a count of five... and as you breathe out, just let anything that is still in your awareness just drift away. That's right. Take about ten deep, refreshing, relaxing, calming breaths, and you will find yourself truly connected to the world, and the Earth, and the Universe... you will feel steady, stable, grounded, at peace....

And breathe again, another deep, relaxing, calm beautiful breath. Feel the oxygen come into your body, and make its way to your brain.

Now just find a spot on the wall just above your line of vision. As you focus on that spot, just let your vision relax and become a little unfocussed. Let your vision spread out a little, so you become aware of even more of the room, and in this wonderful relaxed state, let your awareness spread out and around you, becoming more aware of the room now, letting your awareness stretch out to the side, so you become aware of more objects that you could see before... and almost being able to sense what's going on behind you now.

And now you can close your eyes. Just let the temperature in the room support you in going into trance and helping you become even more relaxed....

Now I just going to ask you to tense and relax different parts of your body. First of all, simply tense the muscles in your feet, and your ankles curl your toes up and tense... tense... and relax now, letting that relaxation flood through your feet and to your ankles... now tense your leg muscles... tense... tense... and now just relax and let that relaxation spread all the way from your thighs down to your calves, leaving your legs feeling totally relaxed, so relaxed that you don't know if you can move your legs at all... and it's OK, because you don't even want to try.

Now tense your chest, and your abdomen... tense... tense... and relax now, letting a beautiful warm feeling of relaxation flood through your torso from deep in your stomach, just flowing gently out, warming you from the inside out...

And now you can simply just tense your hands... tense... tense... and relax them now, just let that feeling of relaxation flow over your hands, feeling good to be so relaxed. Now tense your arms and your shoulders... tense... tense... and relax them now, feeling that feeling of wonderful deep relaxation flow from your shoulders, down your upper arms, around your elbows and your forearms and into your wrists. Just let those arms lie there like limp dishcloths, relaxed and comfortable.

And now tense all the muscles in your face... your jaw... your eyes and the muscles around your eyes... just direct your attention to the muscles round your eyes for a moment, and tense... tense... and then just let it all go, just let yourself relax... let your head go limp.

Now we're going to put it all together... tense your arms, your legs, your body, your head, your jaw, your eyes.... And just hold that moment of tension.... And hold it again.... And hold it.... And then just let go... let it all go and just relax....let that feeling of relaxation just wash up and down your body. It feels so good...just let yourself go limp and relax every muscle in your body.

Drifting, dropping, dreaming, falling.... So much peace and relaxation that nothing else seems to matter to you right now.

I'd like you to just imagine a beautiful beam of white light shining down on the top of your head. Just enjoy that beautiful feeling of light shining down on you, warming you slightly. Let that feeling of radiance just drift gently over the rest of your body, enveloping you in a warm cloak of loving energy. Enjoy the feeling of warmth as it reaches over your entire body feel the warmth and surge of calm, hypnotic, relaxing energy...let that feeling of hypnotic calm just relax each and every one of your muscles... it feels so good, doesn't it, so relaxing, so easy.

[GOING DEEPER]

Maybe you're walking along a wonderful, peaceful beach, enjoying a wonderful warm, sunny day, with the sound of the waves breaking gently on the shoreline. You can hear the whisper of the leaves in the trees, and in the distance the tropical sound of cicadas in the leaves. The sun is just setting, and a beautiful orange glow spreads across the skyline as the most beautiful sunset you have ever see lights up the evening sky. You come to a little stream, burbling and babbling as it finds its way down to the sea. You decide that you're going to follow the stream as it leads inland, and as you follow the stream you come to a set of ten beautiful stone steps, with little lights by the side to guide your way down. You decide to follow these beautiful steps, and you step slowly down each one. By the side of the steps are beautiful flowers, and the gorgeous scent of the flowers just wafts about you dreamily as you slowly step down one by one. 10... 9... 8... 7... 6... 5... 4... 3... 2... 1... last step now... zero... at the bottom now, you see a beautiful mossy stone, worn smooth by the people who have rested on it before... so you decide to simply spend a few moments resting by that beautiful rock and enjoying a few minutes of well earned rest and relaxation in that beautiful grove, warmed by the summer sun and so, so peaceful..

[CONVINCERS]

And as you rest there, completely at peace and totally relaxed, you decide to check if you are really hypnotised – and you are, aren't you. It doesn't really matter, of course, it's all OK. So, putting all your attention on the relaxation on your eyes, you deepen that relaxation even more... too tired and too relaxed to even bother to try to open them, you try and open your eyes, and find with some amusement that you cannot. Don't even try any more, it's OK, just let the relaxation around the eyes double as you relax even further.

As you rest there, you become aware of a wonderfully relaxing and tingling feeling on your scalp. It feels so good as it drifts up and down you forehead, over the crown of you head, and down the back of your neck. It's OK if you can't feel this, though, because that means that you are too relaxed already.

[SESSION GOAL – insert here what you are looking to achieve]

[COMING BACK]

Having experienced a wonderfully relaxing time in that beautiful glade, you decide that you will leave, although you know that you will be back soon to enjoy that wonderful, tranquil energy. As you get up to leave, you take a look around and enjoy the wonderful feelings of tranquillity and peacefulness, and you enjoy the feeling of being at rest and at peace. As you look around you find guideposts and markers that will make it so easy to return to this place in future, at any time you need to relax.

So, one by one you make your way back up the stone steps... 1... starting to feel a little bit more awake right now... 2.. 3.. starting to move your fingers and toes.. 4..5.. feeling coming back into your arms and legs... 6..7.. your mind is becoming clear now, wonderfully refreshed... 8.. coming wide awake now.. 9.. 10.. feeling fully alert and wide awake now.

AUDIO SUPPLEMENTS

I know that it often helps, particularly when you're learning something new, to have someone guide you through it. An old teaching philosophy is to

Demonstrate it

Show them how to do it

Help them to do it themselves

Watch them do it

Let them do it on their own

Now, much as I'd like to work with each of you individually, it's not really going to be practical (sorry!) so I put together an optional audio programme to guide you through. You don't need it to use this manual – and it will help you when you're learning.

Listening to this audio programme will help you understand the process – and what's more it will link up a feeling of being relaxed to the sound of my voice, so that you'll be able to link up pictures, sounds and feelings to get a real total hypnotic experience.

As well as my voice I have got a great relaxing soundtrack to boost the hypnotic experience.

The audio programme is available as a series of MP3 downloads for you to use on your computer, your iPod or your MP3 player – or for you to burn to an audio CD if you wish. Having it as a download means you can get hold of it instantly and that will really help your learning experience. Go to

www.hypnotic-change.co.uk/FreeYourMind/download.html

to get your copy.

The download contains:

> An introduction to Hakalau

> Intro to hypnosis sessions

Hypnosis sessions:

> A hypnosis session with music

> A hypnosis session without music (so you can use your own)

And then the components of the hypnosis programme so that you can use them as you wish:

> The hypnotic induction

> Hypnotic deepeners

> Hypnotic convincers

> Confidence affirmations (as an example of end result imagery)

> Setting a trigger for future self hypnosis

> Return to the waking world

These last 6 are all separate tracks, so you can use them as you wish – you might, for example, want to create your own programme using the *induction, deepeners, convincers* and *return* to use on its own to help you go into trance easily, or you might want to replace the affirmations with your own affirmations instead.

There are more hypnotic programmes available at www.hypnotic-change.com too, and we are working on more being added all the time. You can join our newsletter 'Exploring the Adventure' (see www.heartstorm.org) to be notified of more as they become available (and we're really open to suggestions too). We can also create custom programmes to your requirements.

Chapter 24

GOAL SETTING

Neuro-Linguistic Programming has lots to say on how to structure your goals such that they are readily achievable.

Making sure that goals are 'SMART'

S-M-A-R-T asks questions on your goals to make sure that you've set them effectively – because when a goal has been created properly, then actually carrying it out becomes easy. Well, easier.

By the way, if you've come across S-M-A-R-T before – mine are maybe slightly different from what you might have heard before! So here you go . . .

S

Specific – make sure that you have detail

Simple – is it easy to understand and visualise?

M

Measurable – what will it look like and feel like – be precise

Meaningful to *you* – do you light up when you think about it?

A

As if now – is it stated all in the present tense?

All areas of your life need goals

Achievable – can you see yourself there?

R

Realistic – is it possible?

Responsible/ecological – is it good for others too?

T

Timed – is there a specific date when you'll have achieved it?

Toward – is it a goal that you *want*, not what you don't want

Creating Achievable Outcomes

When setting a goal, we also look at the "Keys to Achievable Outcomes" to make sure that we can achieve the goal effectively and easily. This process is designed to identify what might be getting in the way of any goal and ensure that you can achieve it effectively... so obviously you want to give yourself the best possible chance of being incredibly successful in your business.

So here are the questions for 'Achievable Outcomes'

Key	Question to ask
State in the **positive**	What specifically do you want?
Specify the **present situation**	Where are you now in relation to the outcome?
Specify the **outcome**	What will you see/hear/feel etc when you've achieved this?
Specify **evidence** procedure	How will you know you've achieved this?
Is it **compatible** with the rest of your life?	What will this outcome get for you or allow you to do?
Is it **self initiated** and **self maintained**?	Is it only for you?
Is the **context** appropriate?	Where, when, how and with whom do you want to achieve this?

What **resources** do you need?	What do you have now, and what do you need to get your outcome?
	• Have you ever done this before?
	• Do you know anyone who has?
	• Can you act as if you've achieved this?
Is it **ecological**?	• For what purpose do you want this?
	• What will you gain or lose if you have it?
	• What will happen when you get it?

ABOUT THE AUTHOR

Tim Hodgson believes that everyone has the resources inside to be truly successful and achieve every one of their goals and dreams. He is a Certified NLP Trainer, NLP Master Practitioner, Master Hypnotherapist and Accredited Coach, with a passion for bringing out the absolute best in those he works with.

He works with individuals and organisations to challenge, coach and develop them either working one to one as a coach and therapist, or through training programmes using NLP & hypnotherapy techniques – and a good slice of practical experience.

He is a member of the British Board of Neuro-Linguistic Programming and the International Medical and Dental Hypnotherapy Association, and a Member of the European Coaching Institute. He has trained with a number of UK and America's top leaders and personal development experts, including Topher Morrison, Curly Martin, Tony Robbins, Neale Donald Walsch, Joe Vitale & Roy Martin. He also works in partnership with experts across the country to create massive life change for his clients.

Tim is the author of 'Jump Start Your Coaching Business', a fast start guide to creating the business of your dreams, and a wide range of personal growth and spirituality products.

Tim lives in East Northants, UK, with his two sons. He is also a dedicated martial artist, with a second degree black belt in traditional shotokan karate, and is a passionate skier and snowboarder.

Contact Tim through info@heartstorm.org or in the UK on 08456101460 (Local call rate). Web www.heartstorm.org